KT-512-031

DEAD FAMOUS

BOUDICA
AND HER BARMY ARMY

by Valerie Wilding
Illustrated by Clive Goddard

Hippo

For my long-time friend
Jean Hemming
with love

Scholastic Children's Books,
Euston House, 24 Eversholt Street,
London, NW1 1DB, UK
A division of Scholastic Ltd
London ~ New York ~ Toronto ~ Sydney ~ Auckland
Mexico City ~ New Delhi ~ Hong Kong

Published in the UK by Scholastic Ltd, 2005

Text copyright © Valerie Wilding, 2005
Illustrations copyright © Clive Goddard, 2005

10 digit ISBN 0 439 96357 5
13 digit ISBN 978 0439 96357 2

Typeset by M Rules
Printed in the UK by CPI Bookmarque, Croydon, CR0 4TD

12 14 16 18 20 19 17 15 13

Papers used by Scholastic Children's Books are made from wood
grown in sustainable forests.

INTRODUCTION

It's nearly 2,000 years since Boudica was born, yet everyone knows her name. The flame-haired queen who tried to rid Britain of the Roman invaders is dead famous. Just ask the family…

SHE WAS BIG, GORGEOUS AND TOUGH AS OLD BOOTS.

HER CHARIOT HAD SPINNING KNIVES STICKING OUT OF THE WHEELS. SLASH! SPURT!

SHE SHOWED THE ROMANS WHO WAS BOSS.

Well, maybe…

Boudica was big all right – we know that from the writings of Dio Cassius, a Roman historian.

Boudica rode in a chariot. We're pretty sure the wheels weren't fitted with spinning knives, though. The warriors fighting alongside wouldn't have thanked her for that.

And Boudica certainly took on the might of the greatest power in the world at the time. Rome! But there was more to her life than that. Did you know that Boudica...

- left home for seven years when she was still a child
- became the teenage queen of a Celtic tribe
- gathered together the biggest army ever seen in Britain
- collected human heads as war trophies?

The Romans didn't know what they were in for when they upset Boudica. But she showed them. And the rest, as they say, is history. But is it the history we think we know? Very little has been recorded about Boudica's life, but there were books written soon after her death which told her story. These can help us work out what probably happened.

Read on, and find out what made Boudica the amazing woman she was. Discover the news of the day in the *British Bugle*, and get the Roman point of view in the *Roman Messenger*. Peep into Boudica's secret diary, and see how she might have recorded her private thoughts. Follow the Celtic Britons on their rebellious tour. Check out 'Celtic lore' to discover a little more about the ancient Brits. Learn how the Romans fared when they made the mistake of underestimating Boudica and her barmy army.

BOUDICA'S WORLD

At the time Boudica was born, the Celts had been living in Britain for more than 500 years. Their name, Celt, comes from a Greek word: *Keltoi*, but the first time they appear in history is in the 8th century BC, around Austria, as miners – of salt. Salt was a highly valued item, and the Celts traded it wherever they could. People used to preserve their meat with salt to stop it from going bad – handy in a long, hot summer.

These European Celts were farmers, and used iron to make good tools to help them work the land efficiently. People who farm well, eat well, and they became strong and healthy. So the population expanded. Only so much food can be grown in an area of land, and soon the population grew too large for the land to support it. Some of the younger, fitter Celts began to move away, looking for new lands to farm. They gradually spread across Europe, to Turkey, northern Italy, France, Spain, Ireland – and Britain.

The Celts who settled on the mainland of the British Isles were the new Britons. Yet though they all shared the same culture and background, the Celts never considered themselves to be united as one people. They were divided into various groups, or tribes, and there were definite differences between them. Language, for instance. Each tribe had its own version, which must have been a sure-fire way of spotting a stranger.

Tribal troubles

The Celts gradually spread across the land, and the different groups laid claim to their own tribal territories. They fought each other, and squabbled over who could live where, until finally boundaries were vaguely agreed and the tribes settled down to life in their new country.

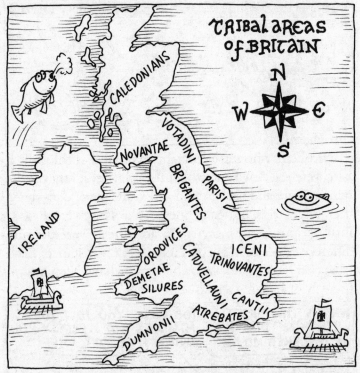

So there they were, peacefully farming the land. Well, maybe it wasn't quite so peaceful. Even though they were all Britons now, the Celtic tribes still had the occasional squabble. It might be a dispute over someone pinching a piece of land, or being suspected of the crime of horse rustling.

Celtic lore
Horse sense

Horses were taken very seriously by the Celts. They were valuable possessions – virtually cash on legs – and were bred, bought, sold and swapped for goods. People used horses for:

- travelling
- riding to battle
- pulling chariots and carts
- racing
- jolly rides in the countryside

We know how important horses were, because some tribes put images of them on their coins. There was even a horse goddess – Epona. She was believed to help anyone who worked with horses, and that included most Celts.

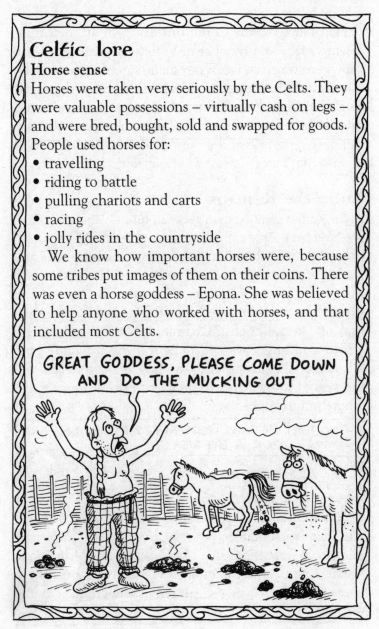

GREAT GODDESS, PLEASE COME DOWN AND DO THE MUCKING OUT

Don't imagine the Celtic Britons spent all their time sowing seeds and squabbling. These guys never forgot they were warriors, too. They made sure they were well-trained and battle-ready. Border skirmishes were one thing but, more importantly, they knew they had to be prepared for a foreign army to come charging over the hill, waving swords and shouting, 'Batter the Brits!'

And that's more or less what happened.

Enter the Romans

In 55 BC, the great Roman general, Julius Caesar, invaded the land his people called Britannia. He planned to crush the tribesmen who were helping his enemies in Gaul. Caesar approached the town of Deal on the Kent coast with 10,000 Roman soldiers. Somehow, the Britons got wind of this invasion – perhaps a fishing boat had spotted warships in the English Channel – and a huge mass of armed and angry warriors was waiting for him. The Romans couldn't get their boats close enough to land on the beach, so they had to jump into the sea and wade ashore in full armour.

Caesar's army managed to win that first battle but, with his ships badly damaged in foul, stormy weather, and his men really fed up, he could see that this probably wasn't the best time to conquer Britain. He decided to cut his losses, and the would-be invaders turned tail and headed across the English Channel to Gaul, the country known today as France.

ROMAN WHO'S WHO

Gaius Julius Caesar

Born about 100 BC. A successful and well-respected soldier, who was made governor of Roman provinces (territories) in Italy and Gaul. Conquering new lands was his big thing.

After a great military career, and a romantic fling with the Egyptian queen, Cleopatra, he ended up as the sole ruler of Rome. Not everyone was thrilled by his management skills, however, and in 44 BC he was murdered by a group of conspirators who thought he was getting too big for his boots.

He's back!

A year later, in 54 BC, Caesar had another go at taking over Britain. This time he brought more than 30,000 men and 800 ships. He could hardly fail, he reckoned – it would take some storm to knock that lot out.

Caesar conquered big bits of the south, crossed the River Thames and found the Trinovantes tribe positively welcomed him. They'd been getting grief from the stroppy Catuvellauni tribe for years. If they cooperated with the Romans, they reasoned, they'd earn a bit of protection.

13

Everyone Caesar conquered had to agree to pay tribute to Rome. That didn't mean saying nice things about the city – it meant sending them money or goods. This would earn them the right to live in peace, and also to enjoy the protection of the Romans.

Once the weather turned cooler, Caesar and his men went back to Gaul. Apart from paying an annual tribute to Rome, the Brits were left to themselves. But that wasn't the last they saw of the Romans. Seventy years later, in AD 16, a group of Britons spotted Roman ships in the English Channel.

14

A full-scale invasion must have seemed less and less likely to the British people now that the Romans seemed to be turning their attention elsewhere. Italy was so far away that the Brits probably didn't expect that they and Rome would have much to do with each other.

Yet, 14 years later, a baby was born who was going to change – or end – thousands and thousands of Roman lives.

The proud parents[1] are delighted to announce the birth of a baby girl.

When: The day it rained till sunset and we found a dead bird in the well.[2]

Where: In the back of the roundhouse.[3]

Weight: About the same as a month-old piglet.[4]

Appearance: Already has a little ginger fuzz on her head.[5]

Name: Boudica.[6]

1 The Celtic Britons didn't keep anything in the way of records. That's because they had no method of writing. So nobody knows who Boudica's parents were, or if she had any brothers or sisters.

2 Boudica was born in about AD 30. Because there are no written records from her time, we don't know if the Celts had names for their days.

3 There weren't any hospitals 2,000 years ago; at least, not in the wilds of Britain. Boudica's mother would have given birth in her own home, attended by friends and relatives. Having babies was a hazardous business, and many women never survived childbirth.

4 Historians tell us that Boudica grew to be very tall, so she was probably a big-boned baby right from the start – quite an armful.

5 Dio Cassius wrote that Boudica's long red hair fell to her hips. As she was so tall, that must have been quite a mane.

6 The new baby's name was Boudica. It comes from a Celtic word, *bouda*, and means 'Victoria' – one who is victorious.

Fireside tales

If the Celtic Britons didn't write anything down, how do we even know Boudica's name, let alone anything else about her?

Like any ancient people, the Brits gathered together around the fire at night to entertain themselves. There wasn't much else to do once the sun had gone down. Children listened to their elders telling stories of great deeds and adventures from the past. When they grew up, they told their children, too. Stories were handed down from one generation to another. It's how the tribe kept their history alive.

No doubt the traditional stories grew and changed. People would add a little, and embroider a little – after all, they had to keep the audience interested. Over time, other, newer stories came along to take their place. So it's likely that the tale of Boudica eventually died out.

But writing, if carefully preserved, doesn't disappear. There may be no British records of the time, but there are some Roman ones, and that's how we know so much about Boudica and her desperate fight for freedom. First, there was Tacitus…

ROMAN WHO'S WHO
Tacitus
Chariot-racing fan Publius Cornelius Tacitus was born in AD 55 or 56, and died in about AD 120. He trained as a lawyer, but soon discovered a talent for writing. The books he's most famous for are his *Annals* – historical records of the Roman Empire from AD 14 to 68 – and the appropriately named *Histories*, which covers the period AD 69 to 96. Tacitus was no slouch. These two books consisted of

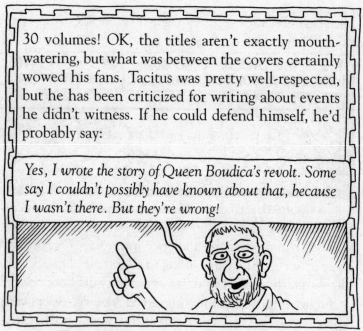

30 volumes! OK, the titles aren't exactly mouth-watering, but what was between the covers certainly wowed his fans. Tacitus was pretty well-respected, but he has been criticized for writing about events he didn't witness. If he could defend himself, he'd probably say:

Yes, I wrote the story of Queen Boudica's revolt. Some say I couldn't possibly have known about that, because I wasn't there. But they're wrong!

Actually, they were right. Tacitus wasn't there, but he knew a man who was. His father-in-law, Agricola, was an on-the-spot eyewitness to a lot of the action, and he filled Tacitus in on the details.

But Dio Cassius wasn't even born when Boudica rebelled…

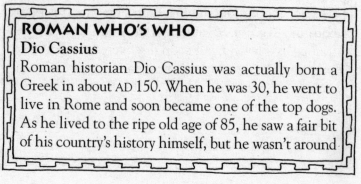

ROMAN WHO'S WHO
Dio Cassius

Roman historian Dio Cassius was actually born a Greek in about AD 150. When he was 30, he went to live in Rome and soon became one of the top dogs. As he lived to the ripe old age of 85, he saw a fair bit of his country's history himself, but he wasn't around for Queen Boudica's rebellion. It's highly likely that he used Tacitus's *Annals* as the basis of his own version, and added some colourful and, let's be honest, fanciful bits of his own.

Hey! Don't knock it! My Roman History *came out at 80 volumes. I was in my 80th year when I finished it — not bad going!*

Neither Tacitus nor Dio Cassius tells us where Boudica spent her early years. She might have been born into the Iceni tribe, who lived in Norfolk and Suffolk, in East Anglia. She might have belonged to the neighbouring tribe, the Trinovantes, who lived south of the Iceni in Suffolk and Essex. Wherever she lived, her childhood was pretty peaceful, give or take the odd border bust-up. Soon there were very few people alive who could remember the Romans' attempts to conquer the country.

But the Romans didn't forget Britain.

HOME, SWEET HOME

In Celtic Britain, there weren't any large towns. Instead there were lots of small villages and farms. People liked to live in groups like this, then they could all help each other. A leather worker might make a harness for someone's horses in return for eggs or barley for his beer. Family members were close. They looked after their old people and nursed the sick. Any old or ill person who had no family was cared for by the rest of the community. There was always someone to fetch wood for their fire, take them meals, and make sure they were safe and comfortable.

Tacitus tells us that Boudica described herself as being of noble ancestry, so we can assume that her family was pretty well-off. She was brought up in a traditional Celtic roundhouse, but it would have been large, by British standards, and would have taken a few weeks to build. Once it was up, though, it would last for years and years.

Some of the people in her village were expert builders, but everyone in the family had to help, too. Roundhouses were built out of materials to be found locally, so first they had to gather everything they needed.

• A tall post, measuring 8 metres, for the centre of the house. That meant chopping down a tree with a straight trunk, then cutting off the branches.

• Long pieces of oak for the roof rafters. Some of those branches would be handy for this.

• Oak stakes to form part of the walls.

• Bendy sticks of hazel for the walls.

• Huge quantities of reeds from the riverside, for thatching the roof. The reeds all had to be cut, tied in hundreds of bundles, and trimmed.

• Home-made rope for tying things together – hundreds of metres.

• Even more twine (thin rope).

• Tons and tons of clay, mixed with dung, for the walls.

How to build a roundhouse

1 You need good grass for your animals, and running water nearby. Avoid swampy ground. Be sure there are trees handy. You'll need to chop down a lot, and you don't want to lug wood for miles.

2 Stick a peg in the ground where the middle of the house will be. Tie a piece of twine to it. Hold the other end of the twine and shuffle round in the dirt, marking out a big circle.

3 Use the pointy bit of a deer's antler to gouge out a trench, following the circle. Take care with the antler.

21

4 Stick oak stakes along the trench to form walls. Leave a doorway.

5 Weave bendy hazel twigs, called wattles, between the stakes. Split more stakes, make holes in each end and slot them horizontally over the upright ones.

6 Stand the large post up in the middle. Anchor it with ropes.

7 Using ropes, pull up the main roof rafters. Tie one end of each to the centre pole, and the other to the wall.

8 Use bendy wood to make two ring beams round the rafters. Then tie crosspieces to the ring beams. That'll stop the thatch falling in.

9 Fix more rafters, then saw off the bottom of the centre post below the ring beams – a tense moment. The house must stand without that support.

10 Back to the roof. Fasten rows of hazel sticks around the rafters, then tie bunches of thatching reeds to them. More hazel rods are tied on top of the thatch, so it won't blow away. Untie the bundles of thatch, then use a tool called a leggat to give it a nice neat edge.

11 The house is waterproof, but not windproof. You must daub the wattles. This is what you need to mix the daub: clay, straw, water, cow dung (the pong wears off after a while). Push the daub right into the wattles. For a great finish, spread more over the inside and outside of the walls. Let it dry. Move in.

Interior design

Boudica's roundhouse would have been warm and dry. Rain just ran off that thickly thatched, steep roof and, once the fire was lit, everyone would be very cosy. The only snag about the fire was that there was no chimney to let the smoke out. It either went out of the door, depending on the direction of the wind, or seeped out through the thatch.

The house was furnished with tables and benches, and had shelves around the walls for storing everything from pots, pans and food to clothes, tools and weapons. By the standards of most people, it would have been quite a posh house. Perhaps Boudica would have enjoyed showing it off.

OUR house

FIREPLACE: COOKS THE FOOD AND HELPS US SEE IN THE DARK. WHEN THE FIRE'S OUT I'M ALWAYS TRIPPING OVER THINGS

COOKING POT: THERE'S NEARLY ALWAYS SOMETHING IN THE POT. MOSTLY PORRIDGE WHICH IS JUST BOILED OATS AND WATER. D.U.L.L.

FLOOR: THE EARTH'S PACKED DOWN HARD, AND WE SPREAD OUT SKINS TO SIT ON, OR WE SIT ON A BENCH

Much of the work involved in running a farmstead like Boudica's would have been heavy, like chopping wood, ploughing and digging. A wealthy family like hers would have had many servants to help run the house and farm. Most slept in smaller houses or huts, but personal servants slept in the main house. Not in quite the same fur-wrapped luxury as the family, though. There was a raised level against the wall of the house where servants could sleep on skins, or even just straw. In winter, they could always move closer to the fire to sleep.

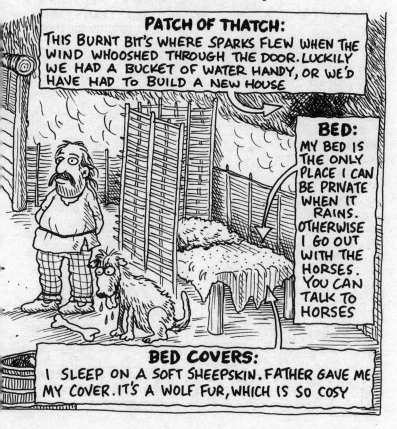

PATCH OF THATCH:
THIS BURNT BIT'S WHERE SPARKS FLEW WHEN THE WIND WHOOSHED THROUGH THE DOOR. LUCKILY WE HAD A BUCKET OF WATER HANDY, OR WE'D HAVE HAD TO BUILD A NEW HOUSE

BED:
MY BED IS THE ONLY PLACE I CAN BE PRIVATE WHEN IT RAINS. OTHERWISE I GO OUT WITH THE HORSES. YOU CAN TALK TO HORSES

BED COVERS:
I SLEEP ON A SOFT SHEEPSKIN. FATHER GAVE ME MY COVER. IT'S A WOLF FUR, WHICH IS SO COSY

Living off the land

Boudica's homestead was completely self-sufficient, and if they ever needed anything they hadn't got, they could trade something, such as one of their horses. No wonder they were so protective of their territory. Land was vitally important to the Britons. Without land to grow food or graze animals, they would starve.

MY HOUSE

RYE, OATS, BARLEY AND WHEAT. SOME TO EAT, SOME TO GIVE SEED FOR NEXT YEAR'S CROP

WELL FOR FRESH WATER

OUR VEG PATCH

HERBS FOR COOKING AND MEDICINE

Boudica and her family ate well. They had a good, balanced diet, and didn't have to go far for their food. It was all around them. Lots of veggies, such as beans, parsnips and cabbages, grew in the nearby fields, all ready to be tossed into the cooking pot.

Boudica's farmstead would have been quite a place to see.

WE STORE TOOLS, MACHINERY AND HAY IN HUTS

FENCE TO KEEP FARM ANIMALS IN, AND WILD ANIMALS OUT

CATTLE, SHEEP, DUCKS, CHICKENS, HORSES

STORAGE PIT

BEEHIVES

WE CUT THE GRASS IN SUMMER AND DRY IT TO MAKE HAY FOR THE ANIMALS TO EAT IN WINTER WHEN THERE'S NOTHING ELSE AROUND

Animal farm

Most families owned livestock, and an important part of their work was looking after the animals. Cattle, horses, pigs, sheep and poultry were vital to their existence, and a family's wealth could be measured by the amount of livestock they owned. Boudica's family would have had rather more than average.

All those animals meant there was a great deal to do each day, so everyone had to do their share. Whatever the weather, the animals had to be fed, watered and kept clean and healthy.

Some animals were more popular than others.

BOUDICA'S GUIDE TO FARM ANIMALS

The first thing to know is that some are sweet, and some are a real pain in the parts. All, though, have their uses. Let's look at the advantages, and a few of the disadvantages, of keeping...

Cattle give milk when alive. When dead, they provide meat and skins for making leather, which is useful for shoes, belts, harnesses, buckets, shields. Oxen are strong, and pull the plough to break up the ground, saving everyone hours of backbreaking work.

Disadvantages: Cows need frequent milking. Can be stroppy in the morning, and fond of kicking the milk bucket over when you've just filled it. Very messy, but the poo is good manure. It stinks, so keep cattle away from your roundhouse.

Sheep give milk and wool when alive, and meat when dead; that's mutton, which needs thorough cooking.

Disadvantages: Droppings aren't easily spotted, but you'll probably be sent to collect them for manuring fields. Spinning and weaving wool is quite a job, but worth it in the long run, especially if someone else does it for you. Sheep bleat a lot for no good reason, so keep them a good distance from the roundhouse.

Pigs' meat is tasty. It's nice salted, too, and keeps a long time. Their manure's good, but smells repulsive.
Disadvantages: The pong, the mess, the bad temper – a pig will happily bite the hand that feeds it. Find a far corner of the compound for your piggery.

Chickens Hens lay eggs, and give lots of feathers for stuffing things and making comfortable cushions and mattresses.

Disadvantages: Eggs can be hard to find, and although hens are easy to catch, we never eat them.

Geese give lovely eggs, and soft feathers.
Disadvantages: Really really really noisy, and can be vicious. Watch your ankles. Like chickens, you can't eat them.

Bees give yummy honey, which is great for sweetening food, especially porridge.
Disadvantages: They sting, and nobody really likes collecting the honey. Don't keep them too close to the roundhouse. It's probably best not to get involved with them.

Horses are all-round useful animals. They aren't killed, but when they die the carcass makes a terrific feast. Their poo doesn't smell disgusting like cow dung. Horses are often nice-natured and they like people.
Disadvantages: Expensive.

As I wrote about the British in one of my books, they do not regard it lawful to eat the hare, and the cock, and the goose. Perhaps they use them in religious sacrifices.

Julius Caesar

Celtic lore
Hunting wildlife

Although there was plenty of meat to be had from farm animals, if your cows were giving milk, and the sheep provided you with wool, it didn't make sense to eat them until they died. It was far better to do a bit of hunting when you fancied a rich meat stew, or a spit-roast. A good-sized wild boar made for an exciting day out for Boudica's family, and it provided a huge feast. There were always deer roaming the forests – they were useful for both meat and skin, and their antlers made handy hooks to use around the house. Any leftover meat could be dried, or salted, so that it could be kept for times when there wasn't much game around. And there were foxes, wolves and bears to hunt for their thick fur pelts. These were vital for the long, cold winters, when extra warmth was needed.

Boudica's family had to plan for the whole year at harvest time. Whenever they could, they ate freshly picked vegetables, but some were stored for use when there wasn't so much fresh food around. The cereal crops were threshed to remove the grain from the husks, then the grain was stored in pits in the ground. The pits were sealed with damp clay, which dried into a crust and stopped the grain going mouldy. It also kept rats out.

Cereal grains were a main source of food for the Britons. They could be ground into flour to make bread, and meal was used in stews and for the thick porridge that Boudica, like most of her people, had for breakfast each morning. Wheat and barley were also useful for brewing beer – a vital ingredient of any feast. The Brits loved a drink or three in the evenings.

Cooking was a skill all women had to learn from a young age. Boudica might well have preferred to be out all day riding or practising sword fighting, but she was a girl after all, and had to learn the skills she'd need to manage her own household. She had to memorize her own collection of recipes to take with her when she married.

POSH PORKY PEASE PUDDING
(feeds the family and servants)

You need:

- WATER (if from the well, check for bugs)
- a bucket of dried peas
- some herbs: thyme and mint, about three sprigs of each
- as much butter as will fit in the palm of your hand (do this before milking time)

- salt
- a large thin cloth
- some flour

What you do:

1 Soak the peas in water all night.
(I forgot to say – start this the day before you want to eat it, or everyone will get very hungry.)

2 Drain the peas and put them in fresh water with the herbs. Boil the lot until it's soft.

3 Drain that water off, too (the pigs will drink it) and squidge the peas through a sieve until you have a nice gooey mass. Mix in the butter and salt.

4 Get the cloth, sprinkle it with flour and put the pea goo on it. Wrap the goo and tie the cloth at the top, leaving a long string.

5 Tie the string to the cooking-pot holder and dangle the whole thing in the pot, which is bubbling merrily over the fire.

Oh, I forgot. You need a large piece of pork, too – that's what should have been cooking in the bubbling pot.

AND THAT'S WHAT MAKES MY POSH PEASE PUDDING PORKY!

ALL CHANGE

Celtic children like Boudica spent part of their childhood with another family. Boys and girls were put into the care of a couple who promised to look after and educate them. For the child, it was like having a second set of parents.

This exchange of offspring helped to cement friendships between families, and between different parts of a tribe – which was very useful in times of war.

We don't know how old Boudica was when she went to her second family. She could have been as young as seven, and it's likely that she would have stayed with them until she was about fourteen. While she was away, she had the chance to meet new people, and learn how to get on with them. She would have known from an early age that this would happen, and would see it as a perfectly normal part of growing up.

BOUDICA'S SECRET DIARY

Spring AD 38

It's nearly here! I've never been allowed to go more than a day's walk from home before. This time next month I'll be off on a real adventure! I'll miss everyone, of course, but my maidservant's coming with me, so there'll be somebody from home. Everything else will be new! New people to play with. And new horses to ride and new places to explore. Oh, it's all so exciting! But it'll be odd not seeing my family for years. Will they recognize me when I come back? I'll be big then. Well, bigger. I'm pretty tall now. I must think about packing. Mustn't forget anything...

✱ Things to take to my new home
Comb – The double-sided bone one
Tweezers – useful for all sorts of things
... splinters, picking bugs out of food
Pin to fasten cloak, best bronze one
Everyday wooden hairpins – must get
someone to carve a couple of extra ones
Twirly enamel hairpin for looking goo-ood
on feast days
Mirror – my beautiful, bestest-ever
bronze one
Pestle, mortar and spoon (I'm going to
wear make-up just as soon as I can, so I'll
need these for my maidservant to make
some cosmetics)
All my dresses
All my shoes
My best plaid cloak
My plain blue cloak
My fur cloak for winter
My best belt with the horse-head buckle
My everyday belt
My special red sleeveless dress (the one
that matches my hair, and has tiny fluffy

FeaTHeRs Round The neck) →
All my undershirts
My bed Furs
Spare clothes For maidservant →
Bed For maidservant? No, she can Find some
STRAW when she Gets THere. ✗

While Boudica was away, she would have learned about the history of the Celts, and of her tribe, and all about their customs and traditions. As she grew up, she would also learn more about her religion.

Ye gods

Since the Britons grew all their own food, their lives were ruled by the seasons. The combination of sun and rain could bring a good harvest, but it could equally bring a disastrous drought or flood. Ruined summer crops meant a hungry winter for farming people, and floods might rot their new plants, meaning a poor harvest next year. Worshipping the right god at the right time, they believed, would ensure a good harvest, or rain at the right time, so it was absolutely vital to ensure that the gods were kept happy.

RAIN, RAIN GO AWAY, COME AGAIN ANOTHER DAY. CAN'T YOU WAIT TILL HARVEST'S DONE? UNTIL THEN LET'S HAVE SOME SUN. PLEASE.

The Britons also made sacrifices to the gods if they wanted a special favour, like making a sick loved-one better. Or they might make an offering of something valuable to say thank you after a happy event, like the safe birth of a son or daughter.

There were hundreds of gods and goddesses to choose from, but most people made offerings to the ones that were special to them.

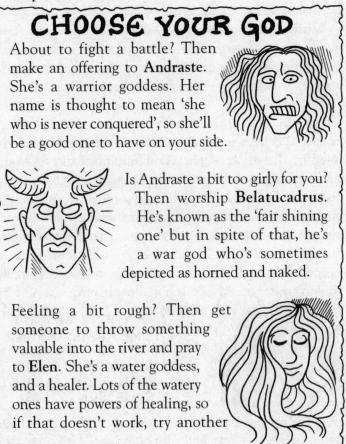

CHOOSE YOUR GOD

About to fight a battle? Then make an offering to **Andraste**. She's a warrior goddess. Her name is thought to mean 'she who is never conquered', so she'll be a good one to have on your side.

Is Andraste a bit too girly for you? Then worship **Belatucadrus**. He's known as the 'fair shining one' but in spite of that, he's a war god who's sometimes depicted as horned and naked.

Feeling a bit rough? Then get someone to throw something valuable into the river and pray to **Elen**. She's a water goddess, and a healer. Lots of the watery ones have powers of healing, so if that doesn't work, try another water goddess, like **Arnemetia**, or the god **Condatis**. For him, though, you'll need to find a place where two rivers meet, so you can't just use any old pond.

If you live around Camulodunum, the war god **Camulos** might be the one for you. Camulodunum was named after him.

And the city of Bath was named after **Sulis**, the goddess of a hot spring, who had the power to heal. The Romans built their baths there, and called the city Aquae Sulis – the waters of Sulis.

The Britons didn't build temples to their gods, as the Romans did, but worshipped them in places that were special to each particular god or goddess. This might be a tree, or by a rock, or on the bank of a river or pond. It might be in the home, on the farm, or on moors and mountains. Some, like the goddess Epona, could be worshipped at many locations. Others were only worshipped in their own unique spirit place.

Mistletoe magic

The more important religious rituals, and very special sacrifices, were carried out by priests called Druids. These were the holy men of Celtic Britain. They wielded a huge amount of power, and had a lot of influence on their king or queen, who relied on them for advice. This advice might be about the best time to attack a neighbouring tribe, or when to sow the wheat – anything that was vital to the people's survival.

Druids held religious ceremonies in small wooded groups of oak trees, called groves.

Celtic lore
Mistletoe

Mistletoe, which had particular magic for the Celts, grew high in oak trees. It was so important in ceremonies that only Druids were allowed to cut it down. To do that, they had to climb up and cut it with a special crescent-shaped blade, called a sickle.

The sickle was made of gold, and using it was a great responsibility. The mistletoe was held in such high regard that it wasn't even allowed to touch the ground. It had to be caught in a white cloth.

QUICK, CATCH THE MISTLETOE!

If you've got the time...

The ideal candidate for training as a Druid was a young man with intelligence, patience and a willingness to learn. The headquarters of the Druid organization was the peaceful island of Mona, off the coast of Wales. It's known today as Anglesey.

WANTED ~ TRAINEE DRUIDS

Young men required for training. If the Druid life is for you, come and study with us.

Set your feet on a career that will support you for the rest of your life. Earn the respect of not only your fellow men, but of kings and queens, too. We will teach you:

Tribal law... You will be given a complete understanding of politics and the law. You will need to act as a judge.

Healing... You will learn to heal by making sacrifices, and by using herbs and other medicines. You will discover how to find or make those medicines.

How to conduct religious ceremonies... You will need to organize festivals, and conduct marriages and other rituals. The secret of mistletoe's power, once learned, must never be divulged.

Sacrificing... You will learn how to sacrifice objects and animals, and how to perform the ritual of human sacrifice (somebody has to do this).

Cursing in several different languages... It is a Druid's responsibility to curse the enemy immediately before any battle.

Dancing... You will learn how to dance in a most terrifying manner in front of your warriors before battle. Naked.

41

Weather control… The secret process of controlling sun, wind and rain involves close observation of the world around us.

Prediction… When your people go to war, you will decide the starting date, and pick the site that will ensure a win. You will advise people on which days are lucky, and which are not. You will learn how to dream answers to problems.

At the end of your training you will be lawgiver, judge, teacher, priest and wise man.

APPLY NOW

But first, answer this question. Have you got 20 years to spare? Because that's how long it will take to train you, and for you to memorize – and we do mean learn by heart – all the knowledge you'll need to become a DRUID.

Apply in person to the Druid in charge of admissions.

YES, IT'S A MAN'S LIFE BEING A DRUID!

SIGH!

Celebrate!

The Druids had four main festivals to organize over the year. They fell at the beginning of each of the four seasons.

Imbolc was celebrated on 1 February, just as the year's new lambs were being born and the ewes were beginning to produce milk. Not only was the flock being increased, but ewes' milk meant cheese for the people as well as food for the lambs.

Beltane, on 1 May, was considered the second most important festival of the year. It marked the beginning of summer, when the animals left the compound and went out to pasture for the coming months. As part of the celebrations, two huge bonfires were lit, and the cattle were driven between them on their way out to graze. This was supposed to protect them from diseases.

Lughnasad, on 1 August, was a celebration of harvest. The crops were ripening and held the promise of a good winter store.

Samhain, on the last evening of October and the first day of November, was the biggest festival of the year, and was the opposite of Beltane. At this time the cattle were rounded up and brought back to the farmstead for the winter. It was a time when the boundaries between life and death were hazy, so people and spirits could visit each other's worlds.

Spring, AD 40

Dear darling bestest family,

I've been away from home for two years now. I do miss it, of course, but I'm having the best time!

I'm taking Boudiga, Goddess of victory, as my own special Goddess, because her name's a bit like mine. Who knows, I might get a chance to fight in a real war one day, so it won't hurt to worship her, just in case. As my maidservant always says, you never know what life's got in store for you.

I did some weaving during the winter, when it was too cold to go riding. I've made some beautiful cloth for a new dress. It's got red stripes going one way, and blue the other, and where the stripes cross it's a luscious purply colour. We're having a feast to celebrate Beltane and I shall wear the dress then. There'll be a huge spit-roast and loads to drink, and lots of music and poems and songs. I'm going to sing and dance all night! One of the women here gave me a brooch she doesn't wear any more, so I shall pin my cloak with that. I've drawn it for you. It's nicer than any of my old ones.

I hope this letter reaches you safely. I will write again next year.
Loads of love. Big hug for everyone.
Boudica

{WEAPONS AND WARRIORS}

From a young age, Boudica had to learn how to handle weapons, and how to be a worthy warrior. Fighting wasn't just for men! If the men were away hunting, it was vital that the women could defend their homes and property.

MUM, LEAVE THE POSTMAN ALONE!

Children learned to use the sword, spear and shield, which were standard battle equipment. We don't know for sure how the teaching was organized. Perhaps women took on the task, but it's likely that all the children in the village where Boudica lived attended a daily 'warrior school'.

prospectus
warrior school

We offer a caring environment for your child.
All battle skills taught.
Wooden replica weapons used for basic training.
We teach use of the

<u>Double-edged sword</u>: slashing, decapitating and
hacking through enemy lines

<u>Slingshot</u>: small stones are
encouraged, for deadly accuracy,
rather than the popular but inaccurate
mini-boulders preferred by young people

<u>Spear</u> a) distance throwing
b) use at close quarters

<u>Dagger</u>: close combat and surprise tactics,
daily practice

<u>Axe</u>: hacking and swinging – we work towards
effective use of the weapon with a single blow

<u>Shield</u> a) for personal defence
b) as a weapon

All weapons supplied. Any pupil breaking one
will be required to carve a replacement.

Boudica learned that it was important not just to *be* fierce when you went into battle, it helped to *look* fierce, too. Surprise was an important battle tactic, and if you could turn surprise into shock, so much the better!

how to dress for battle
war wear for the young warrior

Hair Standard practice is to slosh lime wash through your hair, and dry it in stiff, yellowy spikes. Your tribe will have its own preferred hairdo, but why not dare to be different. Here are some ideas to get you started:

THE HEDGEHOG

THE SPIRAL

THE UNICORN

THE SUNSHADE

Whichever style you choose, remember that the whole idea is to make you look taller, and more fearsome.

Skin You should decorate your body with swirling patterns in blue dye from the woad plant. If you're really, really sure you love a particular design, and will never, ever want to change it, the pattern, or even a picture, can be tattooed on, instead of painted. Better ask your parents first. And check out their own tattoos. You wouldn't want to look the same as *them*, would you?

48

Spears

THIS SPEAR IS LIGHT AND GREAT FOR THROWING AS LONG AS YOU'RE NOT TOO NEAR THE ENEMY. IF YOU'RE UP CLOSE JAB HIM IN THE GUTS WITH IT. EITHER WAY, IT'S BEST TO GET RID OF IT EARLY ON, SO YOU CAN GET ON WITH PROPER FIGHTING.

THIS SPEAR IS SPECIALLY FOR JABBING IN THE BELLY. OR IN ANYTHING ELSE

Dagger Where to carry the dagger is a problem, because you will often go into battle naked. You could always grip it between your teeth, but it might make you dribble, which rather ruins the scary effect you're going for. If you wear trousers, tuck the dagger into your belt.

GOOD IDEA!

49

Sword This is for real fighting! You can go through a whole crowd of the enemy with one of these, slashing and hacking and stabbing and slitting and ripping open. When you get your proper metal sword, you can have a beautiful scabbard like this to keep it nice.

Torc Sometimes this metal torc is all you'll wear into battle. Woo-hoo!

Beautiful, but deadly

Making weapons was one of the most important jobs the local metalworker had to do, and he took great pride in his craft. Weapons were often beautifully decorated, as well as deadly. Some were so magnificent that they were only used on important occasions, for show, rather than fighting.

The metalworker was always busy, because everybody needed at least one blade, even if only for defence. Most people's homes had weapons hanging on hooks, ready to grab at the first sign of trouble. Plain or fancy, all were to be feared.

To: ALL LEGIONS IN BRITANNIA
FROM: ROMAN INTELLIGENCE AGENCY
ENEMY WEAPONS REPORT

CELTS' WEAPONS MIGHT LOOK PRETTY, BUT DON'T BE MISLED. WHEN ONE OF THOSE BARBARIANS COMES AT YOU WITH HIS HAIR ON END, BRANDISHING A SWORD, FORGET ABOUT PAUSING TO ADMIRE THE INTRICATE PATTERNS ON THE BLADE. HE MEANS BUSINESS. THESE PEOPLE ARE A WARRIOR RACE, AND THEY'RE PROUD OF THEIR WEAPONS – LOSING THEM TO THE ENEMY IS NOT AN OPTION.

WE'VE ALL HEARD THE SAD TALES OF THE LEGIONARY WHO LAUGHED AT A BRIT WIELDING HIS SLINGSHOT, ONLY TO BE FELLED A MOMENT LATER BY A STONE RAMMING INTO HIS EYEBALL. THESE MEN ARE DEADLY ACCURATE. THEY MAY NOT BE TRAINED IN THE SAME WAY OUR SOLDIERS ARE, BUT THEY GET PLENTY OF PRACTICE BECAUSE THEY'RE ALWAYS FIGHTING EACH OTHER.

SHIELDS MAY BE MADE OF WOOD, LEATHER OR HIDE. AND YES, YOU CAN EASILY HACK AWAY THE LEATHER OR WHATEVER WITH YOUR SWORD. YOUR ENEMY MIGHT THEN LOOK HELPLESS, CLUTCHING THE TATTERED REMNANTS OF HIS

PRECIOUS SHIELD. BUT BEWARE! THE SHIELD BOSS – THAT ROUND KNOBBY BIT IN THE MIDDLE – COULD STILL GIVE YOU A NASTY INJURY. THE HANDGRIP IS RIGHT BEHIND IT, AND THE BRIT CAN PACK QUITE A PUNCH WITH IT.

SO BE WARNED, DANGER LURKS BEHIND EVERY SQUIRLY-PATTERNED BLADE. BUT NEVER FORGET THAT THE BRITS ARE AN UNDISCIPLINED RABBLE AND TEND TO JUST CHARGE INTO BATTLE WITHOUT MUCH THOUGHT, AND CERTAINLY WITHOUT MUCH PLANNING. HAVE NO DOUBT THAT THESE BARBARIANS ARE NO MATCH FOR THE HIGHLY-TRAINED FIGHTING MACHINE THAT IS THE ROMAN ARMY!

Crafty work

Celtic metalworkers didn't reserve their artistic talents just for decorating weapons. Some of their most beautiful work was in the form of torcs. These chunky neck ornaments were worn in battle, because they were believed to give magical protection to the wearer. They were made of gold, silver or bronze, or gold mixed with a little silver. Some were plain, like curved metal bars, but others were amazingly intricate.

The British Celts loved jewellery…

MEET THE ARTIST

Articus has made jewellery since he was ten. It's a family thing - his father and grandfather were in the trade too.

Articus made this torc by twisting eight gold wires into a rope, then twisting a few ropes together. A little fancy decoration on the ends,

and it's ready for some top person's neck. And if they want to impress their gods, solid gold makes a lovely offering for a sacrifice.

Articus has customers who want a ring for every finger, and some who like a couple for their toes. "I dunno," says Articus, "they'll be wanting bells on them next!"

Articus has a wide range of bracelets and armlets, for ladies and children.

Articus makes dangly earrings and glass bead necklaces in all colours.

Pin your clothes together with brooches by Articus.

They're ornamental and reliable. "Don't want your clothes falling off in the middle of a chariot race, do you?" laughs Articus.

So we can see that the Celtic Britons were not, as the Romans considered them, uncivilized barbarians. They were skilled farmers, hunters, cloth makers, and metalworkers. They looked after their old people, and cared for the sick. They were artistic, proud of their culture, and had a firmly established way of life.

CLAUDIUS THE CONQUEROR

In AD 40, when Boudica was about ten, a Roman emperor called Caligula, who was slightly unhinged, decided he'd have a go at invading Britain and conquering the barbarians who lived there. He was in Gaul at the time, and he marched the army all the way to the coast in the north. When he'd got as far as he could go – to the beach opposite Britain – he ordered his mystified men to stop and fill their helmets with shells. All the shells they could find!

Caligula announced that the shells were the spoils of war – his battle trophies! Maybe he thought he'd conquered the English Channel. Whatever his reasons, it's no surprise that he didn't last long as emperor. He was murdered by his own household guards, and his uncle Claudius became the next ruler of the Roman Empire.

ROMAN WHO'S WHO
Claudius

Claudius was born in 10 BC, the grandson of the wife of the Emperor Augustus, and the nephew of the Emperor Tiberius. He had physical disabilities that made him a figure of fun to the cruel Caligula and, being clumsy and shy, he was something of an embarrassment to the emperor's family.

Claudius may have seemed simple, but he was an intelligent man who loved reading and learning. He studied hard, and wrote books on subjects as varied as history and the game of dice.

When the shock waves of Caligula's murder ran through the palace, the emperor's Praetorian Guard found Claudius hiding, trembling with fear. Those same guards made him their new emperor.

I M-MIGHT HAVE BEEN A BIT OF A SOFTIE AT TIMES, ESPECIALLY WITH MY WIVES, B-BUT I RULED FOR 13 YEARS AND P-PROVED I COULD BE A GOOD EMPEROR. THAT'S MORE THAN THAT L-LOONY CALIGULA MANAGED.

Invasion!

Because people were a little doubtful of his abilities, Claudius decided a successful military campaign was what was needed to earn him a bit of respect. A spot of foreigner-bashing would be just the job. He'd conquer some lands that would bring the Romans lots of riches. Britain was ripe for the taking.

Six steps to a sucessful conquest

1 In with a bang. In AD 43 Claudius's army struck. They landed on the south coast and marched north, fighting and conquering any Brits they met on the way. Several tribes, especially those who traded successfully with the Romans, surrendered, but others fought on, in the true Celtic warrior spirit.

2 Head for the capital. Once across the River Thames, the Romans made for Camulodunum (Colchester). A Brit called Caratacus tried in vain to put up a fight. He managed to escape, and set about organizing resistance against the invaders.

3 Dazzle them with magnificence. With his army, Claudius entered Camulodunum – the head of a victorious force. He figured that a really spectacular demo would show the Brits who they'd tried to tangle with, so he organized a grand parade.

4 Bribe their leaders. Many important people back in Rome reckoned Britain was a good place to invest money in. They sent loads of it, and Claudius shared some of this wealth amongst the friendly kings, to get them on his side. The tribal leaders accepted Claudius's generous gifts without hesitation, and agreed not to fight him any more.

5 Put someone in charge. At Claudius's grand parade, the British kings had to announce publicly to the Emperor that they accepted Rome was their ruler. The new Roman Governor of Britain was to be in overall charge, but as long as these kings – to be known as client-kings – didn't give him any hassle, they'd be left alone.

6 Go home a conqueror. Claudius went back to Rome and had coins minted to celebrate his triumph. He organized lots of fun and games for his people, and planned a huge triumphal arch with an inscription which told that 11 client-kings had surrendered to him.

Boudica was only 13 when this invasion happened. We can't say whether or not she saw Claudius's parade, but it's almost certain that reports of this mighty emperor worked their way across the land. Perhaps Boudica herself passed on the story to members of her family…

Autumn AD 43

Dear Uncle and Aunt,

I've heard such a tale! Roman soldiers have conquered Camulodunum, and Britain is now a province of their empire. To celebrate his triumph, their Emperor Claudius held a parade. But what a parade! First there were soldiers marching, endless lines of them, all in shiny metal armour, and wearing little skirts and boots and helmets. This is what I think they looked like. →

Our warriors would die rather than dress like that! Four of their legions passed through Camulodunum – about 20,000 men.

After them came what they call 'cavalry' - soldiers on horseback, and then the emperor. He can't be all that brave, because he was completely surrounded, they say, by a special group of men called the Praetorian Guard.

EMPEROR

You'd never believe what came next! I can hardly believe it myself. Huge great beasts, each as big as a house! They had thick grey skin, legs like tree trunks, and round feet with giant toenails. Their flapping ears were as big as the skin of a sheep. And - wait till you hear this - their noses hung down to the ground! They're called elephants, and I think they looked like this.

The elephants had men riding on them, who must have been very brave and powerful. I'd love to have a go on one! What a ride! Pass on the news.
Love,
Boudica

It's possible that apart from the rumours, gossip and news about the Romans that spread across the country, life carried on as usual for Boudica. As a young teenager, she returned to her family and faced the change from childhood to adult responsibilities.

Everything was as Boudica had always expected it to be, except that she was now growing up in a land governed by Rome.

A ROYAL CATCH

As she was from a wealthy and important family, Boudica couldn't just start dating a few boys, find the love of her life, get married and live happily ever after. A marriage like hers wasn't just a case of two people getting together and raising a few children. It was a bond between families, even tribes, so it was vital to their future security that she marry the right person.

A couple of years after Boudica returned from her foster family, probably around AD 47, her family found that one special person. And special was the word. Boudica was to marry a king! King Prasutagus!

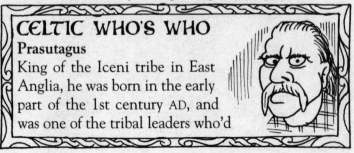

CELTIC WHO'S WHO
Prasutagus
King of the Iceni tribe in East Anglia, he was born in the early part of the 1st century AD, and was one of the tribal leaders who'd

submitted publicly to Emperor Claudius at the Camulodunum elephant parade.

After his submission to the Romans, Prasutagus increased his already considerable wealth because, as a new client-king, he was well-rewarded with gifts.

OK, MAYBE IT **WAS** A FORM OF BRIBE SO THAT I'D DO MY BEST TO KEEP THE ICENI PEOPLE CONTENT UNDER ROMAN RULE.

GREETINGS! MAGAZINE

SPRING WEDDING ISSUE! TOP PEOPLE! TOP STORIES!

ROYAL WEDDING SPECIAL
By our poshest correspondent, Crorla

In a few weeks' time, gorgeous flame-haired Boudica will become Queen of the Iceni when she marries King Prasutagus. I went to persuade her to share a few wedding-day secrets with our readers.

OUR BEAUTIFUL FUTURE QUEEN

First I asked how Boudica feels now the big day is drawing near. Was that a blush colouring her cheeks, or just the reflection of the simple red plaid dress she wore?

'I'm so excited,' gushed the bride. 'Naturally, I'd always expected to marry a noble, but – a king! Wow! That will make me a queen!'

I looked round Boudica's home. It's comfortable, but let's face it, it's no palace. Will her life change much? There's no doubt in Boudica's mind!

'You bet it will!' she declared. 'I don't know what sort of house the King has. It may be a super-duper extra-special up-to-the-minute roundhouse, or perhaps it'll be one of those odd-shaped houses the Romans like. You know, rectangular.

But it'll be better than this!'

Boudica seems a little vague as to her actual royal duties. 'I don't know what I'll have to do,' she said, anxiously. Then that radiant smile flashed again. 'Wear lovely clothes, I expect, and wave to the people a lot.'

Treading carefully, I mentioned Boudica's reputation for bossiness and being rather, er, rowdy. I wondered how she'll treat her people.

'I'll be kind to them,' she said, looking serious. 'I can be rowdy, I know, but I can behave when I have to. And I'm not that bossy. I wouldn't harm a fly, honest I wouldn't.'

'GREETINGS! readers are dying to know what your wedding outfit will be like,' I said hopefully. But, readers, we'll have to wait. She's not telling, though she did hint that it will be 'stunning'!

Next I asked about that crowning glory of Boudica's – her mass of rich red hair. She looked pained.

'I haven't a clue what to do with it,' she scowled. 'There's just so much. Do you know I can actually sit on it?'

I commented that that must be quite a comfort on cold days. Then, readers, I crossed my fingers and asked a delicate question. Could we come and draw some

pictures of her in her new home? I offered a substantial fee, and held my breath. Would she refuse? Not a bit of it!

'Course you can!' she said. 'I'll let you know when I've unpacked and got everything straight. And I don't want anything for it. But if it would make you feel mean not to pay, which I expect it would, you could always give food and stuff to poor people. See?' she gurgled, 'I'm doing queen things already!'

My lady, we wish you well!

How does a future queen prepare for her wedding?

GREETINGS! *took a peek at Boudica's to-do list.*

• *Get all clothes freshly washed. Maidservant to do.*
• *Everyday comb has three teeth missing. Get someone to carve me a brand-new one.*
• *Get best brooch mended.*
• *Rethread green glass beads. Maidservant to do.*
• *Sort out some nice horses for the journey. Father to do.*
• *Get new dresses made. Maidservant to do.*

GREETINGS! *says: Boudica, you're going to be soooo busy!*

Boudica had to make great preparations for her new life and had to say goodbye to her family and friends. We're not sure how far away her new home was from her old one, but it was unlikely that she'd make many long journeys – if any – to visit them. There were all her belongings to be packed, and then there was the move to the home of Prasutagus.

TO THE LADY BOUDICA

My lady,

I am truly delighted that you will soon be joining me as my queen. Everyone here has heard of your beauty, your magnificent appearance. I am sure you will be comfortable in the royal household, and I have many gifts waiting to surprise you. However, you have never been a queen before, so here are a few thoughts to help you:

- I will welcome your advice, but you will not tell me what to do.
- You will show kindness to our people.
- You will listen to the people's problems and help them find solutions.

• You will see that the sick and old are cared for.

• You will show respect to the Romans, with whom I have an agreement.

• You will put the interests of the Iceni before all other tribes.

• Together we will keep peace among our people, and so prevent trouble with the Romans.

I am sure that you will be a great queen. I long for our wedding day. Until then, dear Boudica, I remain your devoted

Prasutagus (King)

Late spring AD 47
TO KING PRASUTAGUS

My Lord,
Thank you for your letter, which was a great comfort to me. I feel I know you already.

Please be assured that I will do everything in my power to be a good wife, queen and (I hope) mother. I am grateful for your advice, and I promise you I will care for your people as if they were my own – as indeed they will be. I will also respect your agreement with the Romans.

I long to be with you, and I remain your affectionate

Boudica

The wedding of Boudica and Prasutagus would have been a huge affair. It was a chance to show off the riches and power of the King of the Iceni, and the whole celebration would probably have lasted at least a day and a night.

BOUDICA'S SECRET DIARY
Summer AD 47

I'm queen! I'm queen! Oh, what a wonderful wedding we had. There were hundreds of guests from far and wide, even some Romans. Of course, we began with the ceremony, when the Druids made sacrifices to the gods on our behalf. That will ensure a long, happy and fruitful marriage. Oh, I do so want children, soon! We seemed to be feasting the whole time. I can't remember everything that was served, but there was roasted meat of every description, and whole pots full of different stews. I ate wild boar, venison, pork and beef, and some tasty veggies and fruits, too. I drank so much wine and beer that I got quite dizzy at times. We heard tales from wonderful storytellers, and there was music all the while.

I know I looked beautiful. My maidservant had brushed my hair till it glowed as red as the fire, and I wore my finest jewellery, including the most gorgeous new torc, presented to me by my husband. Today I don't look quite as good. I'm having a lie-in.

69

Boudica settled down to her new life, and within a year or two gave birth to her first baby. No record has ever been found of the child's name, but we do know, from Tacitus's writings, that the new heir to the Iceni crown was a girl.

Armless

Prasutagus kept to his agreement with the Romans. He and Boudica kept the peace in their own lands, and saw that the regular tribute was made to Rome – contributions of goods like iron, cattle and hunting dogs that the Romans demanded from their new province of Britannia.

However, not all Celtic tribes were as cooperative as Prasutagus was. There were still small rebellions here and there. Then around AD 50, the Roman governor, sick of constant outbreaks of fighting, decided on a course of action that didn't go down at all well with the Celtic tribes. It was perfectly normal for the Romans to confiscate weapons belonging to warriors they'd just defeated. But now, the word went out: take weapons away from client-kingdoms, too.

A new law stated that it was illegal for the Britons to carry swords, or anything else that could be considered a weapon of war. They were told they could only carry weapons used for hunting, such as small knives.

The tribes affected were, to say the least, appalled and insulted. For a warrior race to have their weapons – especially their heavy, beautifully made iron swords – forcibly taken away, was the ultimate humiliation. They weren't going to stand for it. And what was it all about, anyway? What were the Romans afraid of? That the Brits would go back on their word? They'd played ball with the Romans and had made a formal agreement not to fight them any more. Surely the Romans should consider them allies, not possible enemies. *Were* the Romans afraid of them?

Hassle at the hill fort

The furious British tribesmen grabbed their weapons while they still had them and set about attacking the Romans. We don't know exactly where the fight took place, but Tacitus described it for us:

It was an enclosure surrounded by a crude barrier with an entrance too narrow for our cavalry.

Tacitus was describing a hill fort. Unfortunately, the disciplined Romans well outnumbered the warriors, and the revolting Brits soon found themselves trapped inside the hill fort, surrounded by their enemy. Defeat was inevitable.

SPACE FOR A LOT OF PEOPLE TO REMAIN IN SAFETY WHEN THEIR LAND WAS THREATENED.

THE FENCE WAS MADE OF POINTED STAKES WHICH WERE DIFFICULT TO CLIMB OVER. IF THERE WAS PLENTY OF STONE AROUND, THERE MIGHT BE A WALL INSTEAD OF A FENCE.

THIS WAS THE ONLY WAY INTO THE FORT. THAT MEANT JUST ONE ENTRANCE HAD TO BE HEAVILY GUARDED. EVEN IF THE ENEMY BROKE THROUGH THE ENTRANCE, THEY STILL HAD TO MAKE THEIR WAY THROUGH A MAZE OF DITCHES TO GET TO THE GATE OF THE CENTRAL COMPOUND. AN ENEMY IN A DITCH WAS A SITTING DUCK FOR A BRITON ON TOP OF THE RAMPARTS.

A HILL FORT WAS A FORTRESS AREA, BUILT ON TOP OF A HILL, GIVING IT A GOOD VIEW OVER THE SURROUNDING COUNTRYSIDE. FROM THERE, YOU COULD SEE FOR MILES, AND EASILY SPOT AN ATTACKING FORCE LONG BEFORE IT REACHED YOU. WHEN DANGER THREATENED, THAT WAS THE PLACE TO GO. AND IT WASN'T JUST WARRIORS WHO WENT THERE. EVERYBODY DID. IT WASN'T SAFE OUTSIDE.

THESE RAMPARTS, BUILT OF THE EARTH FROM THE DITCHES PILED UP INTO GREAT BANKS, MADE IT DIFFICULT FOR THE ENEMY TO APPROACH THE WALLS.

IT WOULD BE STUPID TO LEAVE YOUR FARM ANIMALS AT HOME FOR THE ENEMY TO EAT. EVEN IF YOU WON THE BATTLE, WHAT WOULD YOU DO AFTERWARDS FOR MEAT, MILK AND SKINS?

DITCHES WERE ANOTHER OBSTACLE TO MAKE ATTACKING DIFFICULT FOR THE ENEMY.

73

It's unlikely that Prasutagus was included in the members of the Iceni tribe who rebelled, because he got off scot-free and he and Boudica were allowed to continue as client-king and -queen. But many leaders and tribespeople were killed or punished, and the whole business left everyone feeling pretty sick about the way they'd been treated. The actions of the Romans were not forgotten. At night, the tale was told around British hearths, and children learned to be wary of the Romans, even when they appeared to be their friends.

Despite this, life was good for Prasutagus and Boudica.

SPRING AD 50

DEAR FATHER and EVERYONE else AT home,
HERE I am, THREE YEARS INTO my REIGN as
Queen of The Iceni! I'm VERY happy with
PRASUTAGUS. He's a good, honest man, who
really cares for me and TREATS me well.
I manage To look Tidy all The Time (don't
laugh) because That's what The people
EXPECT of me. You mustn't look like
everybody else if you'RE a Queen.

I'VE GROWN To love The Iceni people. They
seem To like me, Too. And GUESS what! You
will become a GRANDFATHER FOR THE SECOND
TIME any day now. Yes! I'm GOING TO have
anoTHER baby. Isn't it EXCITING?

Tell everyone. Just think! Maybe I will have a prince this time!

I'm looking forward to having this baby, and a few more perhaps, and to growing old with my dear Prasutagus.

Lots of love,

Boudica

So Boudica gave birth to her second child. We know that this was a girl, too, and we also know that she didn't have any more children. Tacitus only ever refers to two daughters.

Prasutagus now knew that the royal line was secure. His elder daughter would eventually become queen – if the gods allowed her to live, of course. If they didn't, her sister would reign.

GREETINGS! MAGAZINE

Autumn AD 50

TOP PEOPLE! TOP STORIES!

WE ARE GUESTS AT A ROYAL EVENT!

Yesterday, King Prasutagus and Queen Boudica made an offering to the gods in a special ceremony, attended only by the cream of society. And GREETINGS!, of course!

The royal lovebirds gave thanks for the safe birth of their second daughter (isn't she oh-so-*gorgeous?*), and then asked for protection for her.

The procession followed the Druids to a great, spreading oak tree, where mistletoe grew high in the branches. The people circled the tree, while the chief Druid climbed to cut down the mistletoe and release its magic properties. At the same time, two white goats were sacrificed, to please the gods.

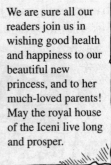

We are sure all our readers join us in wishing good health and happiness to our beautiful new princess, and to her much-loved parents! May the royal house of the Iceni live long and prosper.

A TOWN WITH A FUTURE

When Emperor Claudius first came to power, most people thought him a spluttering clown. However, he proved to be a pretty smooth operator as far as conquering barbarians was concerned, which made him popular with his soldiers and with the Roman people. Then, in AD 54, Claudius died in mysterious circumstances. Rumours soon started flying around.

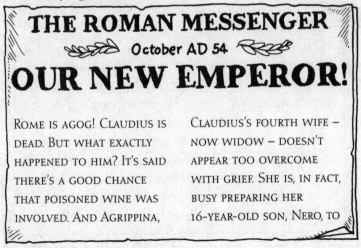

THE ROMAN MESSENGER
October AD 54
OUR NEW EMPEROR!

ROME IS AGOG! CLAUDIUS IS DEAD. BUT WHAT EXACTLY HAPPENED TO HIM? IT'S SAID THERE'S A GOOD CHANCE THAT POISONED WINE WAS INVOLVED. AND AGRIPPINA, CLAUDIUS'S FOURTH WIFE – NOW WIDOW – DOESN'T APPEAR TOO OVERCOME WITH GRIEF. SHE IS, IN FACT, BUSY PREPARING HER 16-YEAR-OLD SON, NERO, TO

TAKE OVER FROM HIS STEPFATHER.

THE GOSSIP RAGING BEHIND CLOSED DOORS (IT'S SAFER THERE) IS HOW ODD IT IS THAT ANYONE WHO STOOD THE LEAST CHANCE OF SUCCEEDING CLAUDIUS AS EMPEROR MYSTERIOUSLY DIED BEFORE HE DID. EXCEPT NERO.

WHAT SORT OF AN EMPEROR WILL THIS IDLE, PLEASURE-SEEKING YOUNG MAN MAKE? NO DOUBT NERO'S MOTHER, WHO HAS ALWAYS DONE EVERYTHING FOR HIM, WILL KEEP A CLOSE EYE ON HIM, AND WILL MAKE SURE EVERYTHING TURNS OUT TO HER LIKING.

WATCH OUT FOR MUMMY'S SPECIAL WINE, NERO…

ROMAN WHO'S WHO
Nero

Nero was born in AD 37. When he was 12, his mother Agrippina married Claudius and persuaded him to adopt her son. She worked hard to ensure that Claudius named Nero as his successor.

The beginning of Nero's rule was successful, because he had a good set of advisers. However, he soon became more interested in having a good time than working for Rome. He loved singing, acting, poetry, women and chariot-racing.

Nero was also cruel. However, the army revolted against him because of his extravagance and crazy behaviour, and sentenced him to be crucified. Once Nero realized that everyone had turned against him, even his private bodyguard, he killed himself.

Shopping centre

Under Claudius, the Romans had established a *colonia* at Camulodunum, known today as Colchester. This was a permanent place for ex-soldiers to retire to when they'd finished their army service. It wasn't just a kindness on behalf of the governor. Having all these highly-trained ex-servicemen handy meant that if there was a sudden uprising by the native Britons, there'd be a very useful army already in place.

The increase in population changed Camulodunum beyond recognition. The Romans who settled in the *colonia* built rectangular houses with wooden frames filled in with wattle and daub, then plastered and painted. The town streets criss-crossed each other in nice straight lines, making it easy to find your way about.

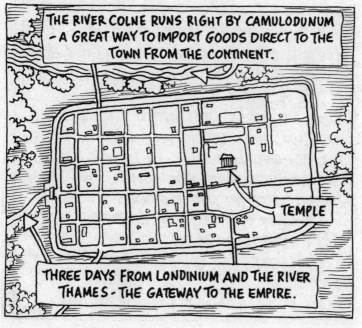

THE RIVER COLNE RUNS RIGHT BY CAMULODUNUM – A GREAT WAY TO IMPORT GOODS DIRECT TO THE TOWN FROM THE CONTINENT.

TEMPLE

THREE DAYS FROM LONDINIUM AND THE RIVER THAMES – THE GATEWAY TO THE EMPIRE.

Camulodunum had a forum – a large open space surrounded by shops, town buildings and workshops. This was where the market was, and where people caught up on the latest news and gossip, and did their shopping. Pottery from all over the Empire was available, and glassware, too, and oil lamps in many different styles. Some of the goods were simple and cheap for everyday use, but others were exquisitely designed.

New importing businesses sold spices such as coriander and dill, wine, and fruits such as olives, dates and juicy figs. British oysters were highly prized by the Romans, who considered them top quality, but their favourite fishy food was an extremely smelly sauce called garum, which they imported in vast quantities. As it needed plenty of sunshine for its production, garum was made in countries with a hotter climate than Britain's.

HOW TO MAKE GARUM

You will need: Some fish. Sardines are good, but any old bits will do – tails, innards, heads.
A LOT of salt.
Some nice herbs. Ones with a strong smell are good, and a strong flavour's even better.
A large container.
Extremely tolerant neighbours.
Method: Mix the fish and herbs together.
Put a layer of fish goo in the container.
Add a thick layer of salt.
Keep layering fish goo and salt until it's all used up.
Leave it out in the sun for several days.

(The strong smell is unpleasant, but normal.)
Gradually it will turn liquid. (It will stink.)
Pound the whole lot together into a thick moosh.
Give it a good mixing every day. (The whole
neighbourhood will stink.)
Lock your door. The neighbours will be
banging on it demanding to know what's died
in your house.

Up for grabs

Of course, many Romans had to grow much of their own
food in order to feed their households, which included
lots of slaves. And for this they needed land. Now that the
cruel Nero was in power, the Romans behaved much more
ruthlessly towards the local people than they did under
Claudius. If they wanted land, they simply drove the native
Britons from their homes and farms, and even kept some as
slaves. Some of the Romans became farmers, while others
ran businesses or shops. They used British slaves to do the
work. Naturally, this was not a popular move.

What the Romans wanted, they took. If they needed
to use force, they did. Argumentative Brits were a ready
source of slaves. Anyone who tried to thwart the Romans
paid a heavy price. Skulls of rebellious Brits were speared
on poles and displayed in public as a warning to anyone
who might be difficult.

Building to impress

And, as if to put their mark firmly on Camulodunum, the
Romans began to build a temple. Now that Claudius was
dead, he'd be declared divine, or godlike, as was usual

with past emperors. This temple would be dedicated to him, and known as the Temple of Claudius. It was to be built of stone, which would be strange enough to the native Britons, who were used to wooden houses, or wattle and daub. But it would also be bigger than any building they'd ever seen. The Temple of Claudius couldn't fail to impress the British people, the Romans felt. This, the grandest building ever seen, was going to stand for hundreds of years. A monument to the power that was Rome!

THE TEMPLE OF CLAVDIVS

TILED ROOF

20 METRES HIGH
45 METRES DEEP
24 METRES WIDE

MARBLE-FACED WALLS

THE GREAT HALL INSIDE CALLED A CELLA

The Romans knew the temple would cost a fortune to build, but they had it all worked out. The problem of raising money for the materials – scaffolding, stone, marble, metalwork, statues, and so on – was solved by taxing the local Trinovantes people. Then they cut costs by using British slaves to dig the three massive trenches needed for the supporting foundations, and to mix the mortar to hold the building stones together.

HUGE BRONZE DOORS, GOOD STRONG LOCKS TO KEEP RIFF-RAFF OUT

NO BUILDINGS NEARBY – EASIER TO FOIL GRAFFITI ARTISTS

PILLARS – ONE METRE THICK

SHADY AREA HELPS KEEP HEAT OFF THE ENTRANCE

GUARDS TO MAKE SURE EVERYONE BEHAVES

STATUE OF CLAUDIUS

So there was Camulodunum, populated by Romans, who were using British slaves and money to make it their own town. The Temple of Claudius was, to the native people, a huge symbol reminding them that they were second-class citizens in their own land. The Romans came first in everything.

Present problem

But around AD 59, the Romans who'd invested money in turning Britain into another province, suddenly decided they'd rather have their money back. Nero was quite a spender, and was constantly short of ready money. Maybe he'd been leaning on his officials in Britain to send more cash home to Rome.

The Roman procurator – the person who dealt with all the government money – was a man called Catus Decianus.

ROMAN WHO'S WHO

Catus Decianus

Catus Decianus was the procurator of Britain. His job was to collect taxes from the British people. He managed a team of collectors, run from an office staffed by slaves. He knew exactly who owned what, how much it was worth, and how much they should be contributing to Rome.

Whenever the governor was away fighting a campaign, it was Catus Decianus who was in charge of any soldiers left behind.

Catus Decianus was an unpopular man, perfectly happy to help himself to any little extras he fancied,

and willing to turn a blind eye to any little extra personal collecting his team indulged in.

BRIBES?
WHAT
BRIBES?

BOUDICA'S SECRET DIARY

WINTER AD 59

There's worrying news. Prasutagus tells me that the Roman procurator (Catus Decianus – I spit on his name) is going to all the client-kings and nobles demanding they pay back the loans the Romans made to them. Loans? What loans? I don't understand what he's talking about. How could we have borrowed money from the Romans? In order to borrow something, you have to ask for it in the first place.

The only money or goods we British people got from the Romans were given as presents.

How can they demand a gift back? If I gave my maidservant a present of a pair of pig's trotters three winters ago (as I kindly did), I am hardly likely to expect her to have kept them in case I wanted them back, am I? Although, judging by the smell coming from the back of her hut...

We really should stand firm against the Romans, and perhaps explain exactly what good manners are. They call themselves civilized. I think their behaviour is vulgar and beastly. They go all over the world invading peace-loving people's countries, and taking over. Can that be civilized behaviour? I hope Catus Decianus and his men don't dare to show their faces here. It would upset Prasutagus greatly.

Death in the family

We don't know if Prasutagus and Boudica received a visit from Catus Decianus's men in late AD 59 or early AD 60. It's possible that they did, and were told exactly what they were expected to hand over, and given time to organize it. But something terrible was about to happen in Boudica's life that would wipe all thoughts of Catus Decianus and loans and gifts from her mind – at least, for the time being.

THE BRITISH BUGLE
SpriNg AD 60
A TRIBE IN MOURNING

The Iceni people are deep in mourning. Yesterday, at his home, their beloved king, Prasutagus, died suddenly. He leaves his adored queen, Boudica, and two young princesses. They are said to be distraught, and weren't available for comment.

A source close to the Queen told us, 'Boudica loved King Prasutagus so much. She will never, ever get over this, but we, her people, will always be there for her and her daughters.'

The details surrounding the King's death are confused. One rumour says that he was so angry at a demand for repayment of one of Catus Decianus's so-called loans, that he had a massive heart attack. Whatever the truth of the matter, life must go on, and an Iceni spokesman assured us that his people are confident that the crown will be safe in the capable hands of Queen Boudica, until it is time for the elder princess to succeed her.

Long live Boudica, Queen of the Iceni!

The young princesses comfort grieving widow, Queen Boudica.

It certainly did seem that the Iceni crown was in good hands. Boudica was an intelligent, strong woman, respected by her people and, with more than 12 years experience of reigning, she had learned a lot from her husband. But these were dangerous times. There was a lot of unrest because of the way the Romans were treating the British people. Who knew what was to come? It took all Boudica's courage to face the uncertain future and to take responsibility for her people.

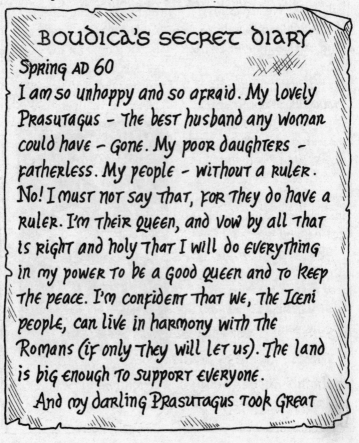

BOUDICA'S SECRET DIARY
SPRING AD 60

I am so unhoppy and so afraid. My lovely Prasutagus – the best husband any woman could have – gone. My poor daughters – fatherless. My people – without a ruler. No! I must not say that, for they do have a ruler. I'm their queen, and vow by all that is right and holy that I will do everything in my power to be a good queen and to keep the peace. I'm confident that we, the Iceni people, can live in harmony with the Romans (if only they will let us). The land is big enough to support everyone.

And my darling Prasutagus took great

care to make sure that everyone is satisfied. In his will, he has left half of all he owns to our two daughters, and half to the Roman emperor. Surely the Romans, especially that beastly Catus Decianus, must agree that this was a very fair decision. I would like to keep the horses, though. Perhaps it would be a good idea to put them somewhere safe before the Romans come to claim their half. And maybe one or two pieces of my favourite jewellery...

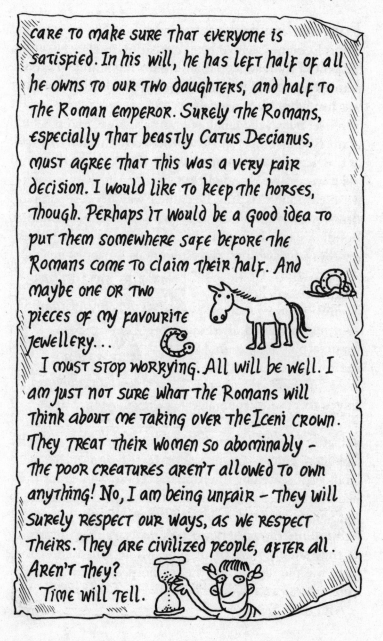

I must stop worrying. All will be well. I am just not sure what the Romans will think about me taking over the Iceni crown. They treat their women so abominably – the poor creatures aren't allowed to own anything! No, I am being unfair – they will surely respect our ways, as we respect theirs. They are civilized people, after all. Aren't they?

Time will tell.

Fury unleashed

Catus Decianus, who'd been expecting to claw back the amount of the so-called loans from King Prasutagus, now realized there was a much bigger prize for the taking. It was just what Nero needed.

He set out to claim half of Prasutagus's wealth on behalf of the Roman emperor. He was perfectly entitled to do so, as this was the arrangement in the King's own will.

However, he decided that half of the King's estate wasn't enough. Catus Decianus was no respecter of British ways, or of Prasutagus's will. He sent his men into Boudica's royal household and stripped it. Clothes, jewellery, furnishings, slaves, animals – everything they wanted, they took. They even claimed Prasutagus's land. When the procurator's men had gathered all they wanted (plus a few items for their own personal use), they allowed their own slaves to go and rummage through what was left over.

Catus Decianus didn't stop there – he was on a roll. The Iceni chiefs – the nobles of the tribe – also had their lands confiscated by the Romans. These were lands that had been passed down through the family from father to son. They were not spoils of war; they were the chiefs' rightful inheritances. But the Romans wanted the lands, so they simply took them. The whole kingdom of the Iceni was plundered, and the relations of the royal family were taken into slavery.

And their queen?

THE ROMAN MESSENGER
Martius AD 60

Procurator Catus Decianus reports that his agents have removed from the Iceni tribe those goods and lands that rightfully belong to the Roman emperor. The so-called Queen of the Iceni, Boudica, was uncooperative, as were her two daughters. They have been punished — in a purely symbolic manner — and it is to be hoped that the Iceni people will learn from the example that has been made of these disobedient women.

Rome is the master of Britannia. No more will be heard of the matter.

The British Bugle
Spring AD 60
INSULTS AND ASSAULT

In a ghastly aftermath to the plundering of the Iceni kingdom, the whole tribe is stunned and appalled at the latest Roman atrocity.

Queen Boudica, still reeling from the shock of the King's death, protested that the terms of his will were being ignored. Her people, she pointed out, were having everything taken from them. How were they to live without land to grow food, or farm animals, or shelter? Were they to be left to wander the country, homeless, without even a hunting knife?

The Romans listened to the Queen's protests. However, instead of joining in a discussion about the situation, they took her and the two Iceni princesses to a public place. There, in an appalling show of cruelty, they stripped Queen Boudica and flogged her mercilessly. Her daughters were also brutally assaulted right in front of her. Watchers said that all three took their so-called punishment with dignity, and that Queen Boudica's face showed no expression throughout the whole ordeal.

So ends the royal house of the Iceni.

In one swoop, Boudica had lost her home, her tribal lands and her crown. But the Romans had made a mistake. They had assumed that Boudica was like their women – conditioned to submit to their master's will.

Not Boudica. They might have whipped her, but she wasn't beaten.

She was angry.

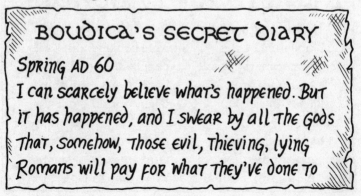

BOUDICA'S SECRET DIARY

Spring AD 60
I can scarcely believe what's happened. But it has happened, and I swear by all the gods that, somehow, those evil, thieving, lying Romans will pay for what they've done to

ME, my daughters, my kinsmen and women, and to my country. They will REGRET the day they EVER CROSSED Boudica, Queen of the Iceni. FOR QUEEN I was, QUEEN I am, and as QUEEN I will die.

I will have my REVENGE.

THE ROAD TO WAR

Boudica acted swiftly. First she had to speak to her people, to convince them they didn't have to sit back and take whatever the Romans threw at them. They could do something about it. She knew she had to rouse them to follow her and fight for what was theirs by right. And she wanted *everyone* to follow. It was time to take Britain back from the invaders.

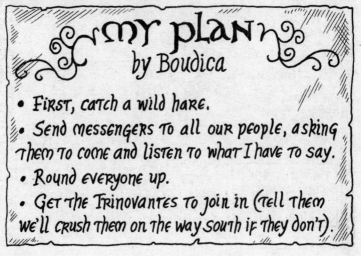

My plan
by Boudica

- First, catch a wild hare.
- Send messengers to all our people, asking them to come and listen to what I have to say.
- Round everyone up.
- Get the Trinovantes to join in (tell them we'll crush them on the way south if they don't).

- Get someone to build a high platform of earth to stand on, so everyone can see me.
- Make speech from earth platform (rest voice for a few hours beforehand).
- Make a new chariot.

Celtic lore

Chariots

Celtic chariots were small, light and nippy; ideal for carrying a warrior into battle. Usually, the chariot held two men, one to drive and the other to fight.

FRONT LEFT OPEN SO WARRIOR COULD LEAP FORWARD ON TO THE POLE TO FIGHT

WICKER SIDES GAVE PROTECTION FROM ATTACK

WOODEN YOKE FIXED TO POLE

TWO HORSES WERE HARNESSED TO THE CENTRAL POLE

WOODEN WHEELS HAD HOT IRON TYRES FITTED TO THEM; AS THE IRON COOLED, IT TIGHTENED, HOLDING THE HUB AND SPOKES TIGHTLY TOGETHER

A warrior might leap out of the chariot and fight on the ground, but his charioteer would be ready to come and scoop him up if necessary. Even in death, a warrior's chariot had a role to play. It would be buried in the grave, either whole and upright, or in bits, with the warrior's body placed on top. Sometimes horses were buried there, too.

YOU KNOW WHAT SLAVERY MEANS. IF THAT LIFE APPEALS TO YOU, THEN PUSH OFF RIGHT NOW AND LET THE ROMANS CAPTURE YOU. BETTER TO BE POOR AND FREE THAN BE RICH, BUT RULED BY ROMANS. REMEMBER THE HUGE TAXES WE PAY. THINK OF WHAT THEY'VE STOLEN FROM US!

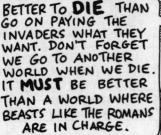

BETTER TO **DIE** THAN GO ON PAYING THE INVADERS WHAT THEY WANT. DON'T FORGET WE GO TO ANOTHER WORLD WHEN WE DIE. IT **MUST** BE BETTER THAN A WORLD WHERE BEASTS LIKE THE ROMANS ARE IN CHARGE.

97

Boudica's powerful speech worked its magic. The Iceni and Trinovantes had experienced the Romans' abrupt about-turn in their treatment of the Britons. They'd seen how brutally the invaders could behave towards an innocent woman and her children, just to make an example of them. When Boudica let the hare loose from beneath her cloak, they watched it run. It fled in the direction the Druids had foretold it should if the war was to be successful. That gave the Celts all the encouragement they needed for the fight ahead. It meant the gods were on their side.

They were ready for Boudica's call to war. Tens of thousands of people rallied to her side, armed to the teeth and thirsty for action. As a true warrior race, they might have appeared to surrender their weapons when the Romans demanded it, but first they made sure they had secret stashes of swords, slings and daggers. Now they brandished them to show the Queen their support for her act of revenge.

So, feeling heartened, they set off behind their leader, Queen Boudica, to face the might of the Roman army. Boudica already had her first target in mind. She was going to the centre of Roman society.

Murder at Mona

Meanwhile, the Roman governor of Britain, Suetonius Paulinus, was determined, as part of the plans to subdue the British people, to deal with what he saw as one of the causes of trouble. He planned to sort out the Druids. But they were a long way away. In the other direction.

ROMAN WHO'S WHO
Suetonius Gaius Paulinus

Suetonius Paulinus was born early in the 1st century AD. He was a very successful Italian general who'd managed to put an end to a fiercely troublesome revolt in the mountains of Mauretania, in North Africa. His reward in AD 58 was the governorship of Britain, where he was kept busy conquering tribes, putting down small rebellions and building good strong forts.

I RECKON THOSE DRUIDS ARE TROUBLE WITH A CAPITAL T. I'M GOING TO HEAD FOR THEIR HQ AND SORT THEM OUT

To Suetonius Paulinus,
with the army in Wales
Early spring, AD 60

Darling Suety,
Where are you? How long are you going to
be away? I miss you so much. What use is
it having a boyfriend who's never here? If
you want to marry me, you must come
back. I can't cope here without you. My
slaves are lazy and I'm b·o·r·e·d. I had my
hair done three times today.
Love from your lovey-dovey girly-wirly.

Spring, AD 60
Dearest,
When will you learn? I am in charge of
the whole of the Roman army in
Britain and I have an important job to
do. We are heading for the island of
Mona, off the coast of Wales. This is
where those wretched Druids train new
blood for their dangerous work – it's
their headquarters. We wouldn't mind
if they stuck to religion, but they don't.

They meddle in law and politics, and in my opinion they're behind most of the grief we get from the Brits. They even cause trouble abroad. Men from Gaul and places even further afield go to Mona to train, then go back and stir their own people up.

They have to be squashed. And I'm the man to do it. What can a few Druids do against the might of my trained men? All we have to do is land on the island and tell them who's in charge. Piece of cake.

Love,

Suetonius

PS Who said anything about marriage? Don't push it or you'll be a lovey-dovey-girly-wirly-gonny-wonny.

A few Druids probably couldn't have achieved a lot against the Roman army, and it's likely that Suetonius Paulinus thought he could simply walk in with his soldiers and overcome any defiance. But it wasn't that easy – he'd reckoned without the rage of the warlike local people. And there were lots of them. Mona was a safe haven for refugees who'd fled the Roman regime, and they weren't going to give up their freedom lightly.

The soldiers built flat-bottomed boats and rowed across the narrow strip of water between the mainland and the island of Mona. The cavalrymen simply rode their horses through the shallows and swam them through the deeper parts.

What a shock awaited them! On the far shore, the British people crowded near the water's edge. But this was no peaceful welcome. The Druids were lined up along the beach with their hands raised to the sky, calling on their gods to defeat the invaders. They cursed the Romans in all the most horrible ways they could imagine.

Women, clad all in black, with their hair loose and blowing wildly in the wind, raced back and forth, waving flaming torches. They screamed and cursed, as if they were possessed by devils.

The Romans froze. They'd never seen anything like this. But Suetonius Paulinus yelled at them to pull themselves together, to move themselves, to get on land and fight. Were they going to be beaten by a band of *women*?

At last the soldiers charged forward. The Druids and other Britons fought savagely, but they were no match for the well-armed Romans, and it wasn't long before those on the beach were slaughtered.

The sacred groves of oak trees were chopped down. No more could Druids hold their religious ceremonies before altars stained with the blood of sacrifice. Mona belonged to Rome.

And then, Suetonius Paulinus received a message.

COME BACK AT ONCE! THE BRITONS ARE REVOLTING.

THIS LOT WERE PRETTY DISGUSTING, TOO.

TEMPLE OF DEATH

We don't know the exact time of year, but possibly in the early summer of AD 60, the enraged Boudica rode her chariot through East Anglia at the head of her army. She was making for the Roman power base at Camulodunum, where the population were going about their day-to-day lives, all unsuspecting. On the way, she claimed her first victims: the Romans who'd settled in the countryside.

BOUDICA'S SECRET DIARY

Summer AD 60

Wow! What a day! We've disposed of quite a few of the enemy – took them completely by surprise! Although it's all been dreadfully tiring, my blood's up. I'm desperate to get on with the journey to Camulodunum, which I like to think of as a town with only days left to exist. But my people are worn out.

Most of them don't have horses, and have to walk, or take turns riding in their carts. They need a rest if we're going to do what I intend. And my poor girls are still bruised and battered from what those filthy Romans did to them. They need to sleep. The scars on my back are healing well but, modern as my chariot is, it's still a bumpy ride, and painful. You'd have to be drunk or half-dead to sleep as it bounces along. More and more fine British people are joining us all the time. We've come across a few Romans who've burst out laughing and called us all sorts of names – they think we're making a big mistake in attacking their town. My army has been called 'barmy', 'senseless', 'crazy', 'mad'... Well, I'm mad all right, and if my army is barmy, I'm proud of every barmy

Ha Ha

man, woman and child. My warriors are the bravest in the world, and there must be at least a hundred thousand of us.

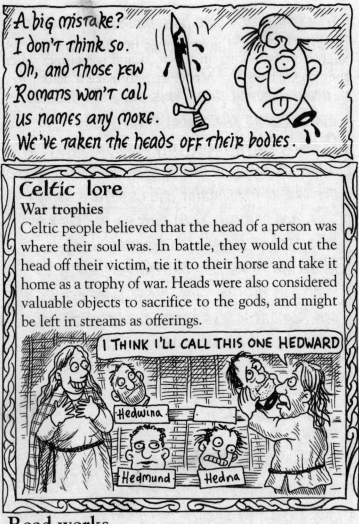

A big mistake?
I don't think so.
Oh, and those few
Romans won't call
us names any more.
We've taken the heads off their bodies.

Celtic lore

War trophies

Celtic people believed that the head of a person was where their soul was. In battle, they would cut the head off their victim, tie it to their horse and take it home as a trophy of war. Heads were also considered valuable objects to sacrifice to the gods, and might be left in streams as offerings.

I THINK I'LL CALL THIS ONE HEDWARD

Hedwina

Hedmund   Hedna

Road works

Wherever they could, Boudica and her army took advantage of the new roads the enemy had built. They were able to keep up a much higher speed than if they'd followed the tracks they were used to.

The Romans believed that a straight line was the quickest way to anywhere. If they came across swampy ground, they'd happily make a kink in the road and sometimes when they met a river it was necessary to make a detour to a shallow part, but otherwise, dead straight was the rule.

HOW TO BUILD A ROAD - THE ROMAN WAY

1 Dig a ditch on either side of where the road will be. Heap up all the stuff you dig out in the middle. That way the road is higher than the ground either side. (It makes a high-way.) Get legionaries and slaves to do the heavy work.

2 Cover the piled-up stuff with stones, then add sand, chalk or whatever's handy in the area, then more stones or gravel.

3 Put some smooth stone slabs on top.

4 Be sure the road surface is slightly rounded, so when it rains the water runs

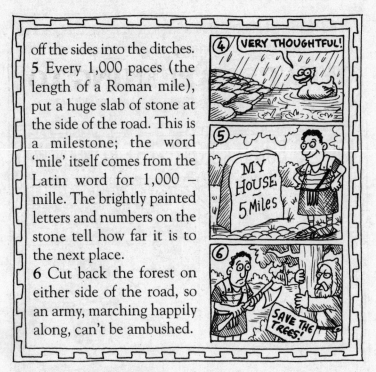

off the sides into the ditches.

5 Every 1,000 paces (the length of a Roman mile), put a huge slab of stone at the side of the road. This is a milestone; the word 'mile' itself comes from the Latin word for 1,000 – mille. The brightly painted letters and numbers on the stone tell how far it is to the next place.

6 Cut back the forest on either side of the road, so an army, marching happily along, can't be ambushed.

Ominous omens

As the rampaging rebel Britons moved towards Camulodunum, they encountered more and more country homes. They burst into farmhouses, looting and burning and murdering wherever they went. Like killer ants, they swarmed over everything and everyone in their way.

Word spread south ahead of them. Something terrible was happening. The Brits were revolting.

At first, the townsfolk of Camulodunum didn't take too much notice. There were always rumours about the barmy Brits. But then strange things began to happen. Things no Roman dared ignore. Were their gods trying to tell them something?

THE ROMAN MESSENGER

Junius AD 60

WHAT'S HAPPENING TO OUR TOWN? DO THESE OMENS SPELL DISASTER?

DO THESE STRANGE SHAPES IN THE SAND MEAN THERE WILL SOON BE REAL BODIES LYING HERE? ROMAN BODIES?

THE CAMULODUNUM THEATRE IS CLOSED. NO ONE WILL ENTER AFTER WILD HOWLS WERE HEARD YESTERDAY, ECHOING THROUGH THE AUDITORIUM. THE AUDIENCE FLED. SUPERSTITIOUS ACTORS HAVE VOWED NEVER TO SET FOOT ON THE STAGE AGAIN.

AND WHAT DO WE MAKE OF THE FACT THAT LOW, BLOOD-CURDLING MOANS WERE HEARD IN THE SENATE HOUSE? THIS HAS THE RING OF TRUTH ABOUT IT – THE LEADERS OF OUR TOWN ARE HONOURABLE MEN, NOT GIVEN TO FANCIFUL IDEAS.

THERE IS NOTHING FANCIFUL ABOUT THE MYSTERIOUS TOPPLING OF THE STATUE OF THE GODDESS OF VICTORY. NO REASON CAN BE FOUND FOR IT FALLING FROM ITS PLINTH, WHERE IT OVERLOOKED THE ALTAR IN FRONT OF THE TEMPLE OF CLAUDIUS, BUT THERE IT LIES. THE

GODDESS'S FACE IS TURNED AWAY FROM THOSE WHO LOOK ON HER, AS IF SHE TURNS AWAY FROM THE ROMAN PEOPLE.

RELIABLE WITNESSES AT THE ESTUARY WHERE THE RIVER JOINS THE SEA REPORTED THAT A WHOLE TOWN COULD BE SEEN BENEATH THE SURFACE OF THE WATER. A GHOST TOWN? A SIGN OF THINGS TO COME? AND, EVEN MORE CHILLING, MEN AT THE COAST HAVE REPORTED THAT THE SEA WAS STAINED RED THIS MORNING. BLOOD RED.

CITIZENS, TAKE HEED.

THE BRITISH BUGLE

SUMMER AD 60

The Romans are jittery today. The sudden and unexplained toppling of one of their statues – the goddess of victory, no less! – has got them all huddling together, wondering what's going on. Add that to all the other weird things that have happened in Camulodunum, like the women who've gone loopy, screaming that destruction is nigh, and there seems to be good reason for them to be so jumpy.

But should we be worrying, too? What do our readers think?

INSIDE TODAY: Romans. Do you love 'em or hate 'em? And does it really matter?

Ready for action

Before long, word reached Camulodunum that an army, led by a wild red-haired woman, was on its way. Everyone in its path was slaughtered and it was heading for the town! The ordinary citizens panicked. Retired soldiers living in the town and those living close by could hardly believe what was happening. Could the Brits really be barmy enough to think they could take on the might of the Romans? And then it dawned on them. There wasn't much to take on. The bulk of the army was away on Mona with Suetonius Paulinus. There were no great walls to keep out an enemy. The town was virtually undefended. They, the veterans of previous battles, were all there was. The veterans decided to send to Procurator Catus Decianus for back-up support. In the meantime they got out their weapons, which had hardly been used since their army days, and prepared to fight.

There was going to be a bit of a tussle, that was for sure – but they'd win, they reckoned. The Romans always won.

Enter, the Queen

The great mass of Britons – the barmy army – moved steadily onwards. It was unstoppable. Camulodunum, with just 700 fighting men, didn't stand a chance. Catus Decianus sent all the men he could spare to help – a pitiful 200. And even they weren't particularly well-armed. The town, with under 1,000 men to defend it, stood silent, waiting.

Then Queen Boudica rode in on her chariot. The silence was broken as the townspeople realized the true horror that was descending on them. Screams and cries for mercy were ignored as wooden shops and houses went up in flames. Rampaging Brits smashed their way through town, swords slashing, fiery torches igniting anything that would burn. People who tried to hide in their homes were routed out and mercilessly slaughtered by blade or fire.

But there was one building in town that wouldn't burn. The great Temple of Claudius was built of stone. The cry went up among those still living. 'The temple! Run for your lives! Run to the temple!'

Shocked Roman soldiers, and terrified men, women and children surged through the huge bronze doors of the temple and barricaded themselves in. There they felt safe from fire and blade. They settled down to wait for Boudica and her army to finish their dreadful work and move on.

last will and testament

of Effra, slave and lady's maid to Livia, wife of Didius the tax collector.

I, who am likely to die soon, leave all my worldly goods to my sister Briga, who lives in Londinium. I don't know who her master is. I send her these words, and hope that some kind soul will find her and give them to her, as I wish her to know my end.

Briga, I'm trapped with a thousand people as scared as I am. We're inside the Roman temple at Camulodunum and are being besieged by Boudica, Queen of the Iceni. You will know of her. She has a mighty horde with her and has destroyed the town. We're waiting in the darkness of the cella — the great hall — and are crammed in so tightly there is hardly room to breathe. That scarcely matters, as the air will soon be unfit to keep us alive. The hungry children's cries grow weaker, and it pains me to see the terror on their mothers' faces. They do not know what will happen to their babies.

I fear that I do know. The Romans among us say that the temple walls have been made far too thick to be knocked down. They are convinced that Boudica is going to try to starve us out. If we hold on, they say, help will arrive, and she will move on as soon as she hears of their coming. I am a Celt, and I know differently. Boudica is a queen, and too proud to accept half a victory. She will get to us somehow. Even now there is such a banging and thumping on the walls that I almost fear the attackers might, by some ghastly miracle, break through.

A soldier has just murmured something about the roof being the weak spot, and that is where he would attack if he were in Boudica's sandals. His words are being passed around, and a new terror is spreading.

Briga, if help does not arrive very soon, the end cannot be long. Goodbye, dear sister. We have not seen each other since our enslavement many years ago, but I have always thought of you daily, and love you still, for you are all I have.

Effra

Siege

The captives waited and waited. For two long days, they held out with no water, food, light or toilets, but with constant prayers for rescue. The noise from people wailing in fear, and from scared children crying, was constantly in their ears. No one could sleep. The heat and the stench from the filth that sloshed over the floor were terrible. But still they waited. Surely that crazed army would leave once they realized that they couldn't break down the mighty doors, and that the walls were too strong for them ever to break through.

But Boudica wasn't giving up. She was not satisfied. Her revenge must be complete. Soon the captives became aware of a new sound. And it was coming from above. A steady pounding.

Suddenly, the people gazing up towards the sound were almost blinded as plaster chunks and dust rained down on them and a shaft of light burst through the ceiling. But this was no welcome light. Above them, they saw the grinning, sweating faces of men who wanted nothing but to kill.

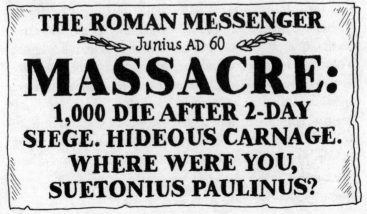

THE ROMAN MESSENGER

Junius AD 60

MASSACRE:
1,000 DIE AFTER 2-DAY SIEGE. HIDEOUS CARNAGE. WHERE WERE YOU, SUETONIUS PAULINUS?

THE BRITISH BUGLE
SUMMER AD 60
HEADS, SHE WINS!

Queen Boudica was triumphant yesterday as her men hacked off the head of Claudius and threw it in the river. 'I'd rather it was his real head,' she told our reporter, 'but this makes a nice offering for our gods.'

Ambush

Suetonius Paulinus was too far away to be of any help. But reinforcements, in the shape of the 9th Legion, rushed towards Camulodunum as soon as their commander, Petilius Cerealis, heard what was happening. The Britons, though, had their spies, who were expecting just such a move on the part of the Romans. They ambushed the legion in a forest. Over 2,000 foot-soldiers got the same treatment as the people of Camulodunum, and the only survivors were Petilius Cerealis and his cavalry. They fled, galloping back to camp, from where the news spread of the flame-haired maniac with the massive, vicious army.

BOUDICA'S SECRET DIARY

SUMMER AD 60

I wish I could say I feel better, but I don't. We've got rid of 15,000 or more Romans and Roman-lovers, but the anger inside me isn't shrinking, as I thought it would. It's growing. I can't believe the hatred I feel for those of my countrymen who live in harmony alongside the Romans. Are they mad? Don't they realize what evil-doers, what thieves the foreigners are? Or are they blinded by their soft living, their luxury, their filthy baths...?

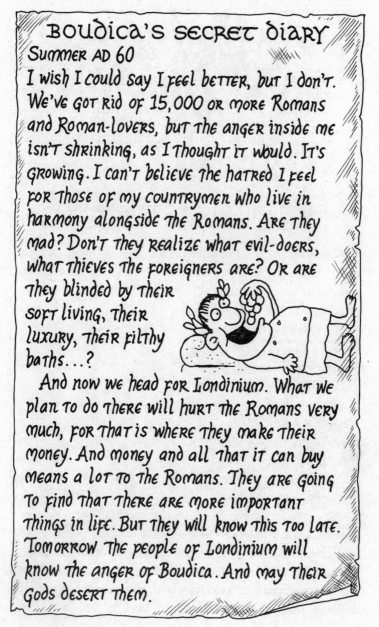

And now we head for Londinium. What we plan to do there will hurt the Romans very much, for that is where they make their money. And money and all that it can buy means a lot to the Romans. They are going to find that there are more important things in life. But they will know this too late. Tomorrow the people of Londinium will know the anger of Boudica. And may their gods desert them.

LONDINIUM'S BURNING

Londinium – present-day London – was only ten years old in the summer of AD 60, but it was already the trading capital of Britain. Imports were distributed via great road links to the rest of the country, and it was a good starting point for exporting to the continent, especially Gaul.

While the streets weren't exactly paved with gold, there was plenty of money to be made in Londinium, so that's where merchants tended to settle. Ships called at the port from all over the Roman Empire, and the unloading and distribution facilities were organized with true Roman efficiency. There was a bridge across the River Thames, giving easy access to the south, while Camulodunum was just three days' march away to the north.

Londinium was rich, and it was growing. It had everything going for it, and many Romans seeking to make a fortune decided that this town held the promise of a bright future. But they were wrong. The future wasn't sunny at all.

THE ROMAN MESSENGER
Julius AD 60

BOUDICA AND HER BARMY ARMY NO THREAT TO LONDINIUM, SAYS PROCURATOR

CATUS DECIANUS, OUR ESTEEMED PROCURATOR, WARNED TODAY THAT BOUDICA, EX-QUEEN OF THE ICENI, IS HEADING TOWARDS LONDINIUM WITH EVIL INTENTIONS. SHE IS AT THE HEAD OF A CRAZED ARMY OF BRITONS, ALTHOUGH, AS CATUS DECIANUS COMMENTED, 'ARMY' IS NOT THE WORD FOR THIS HALF-NAKED, FILTHY RABBLE.

HOWEVER, CATUS DECIANUS ASSURES THE PEOPLE OF LONDINIUM THAT PETILIUS CEREALIS HAS BEEN SENT TO HEAD OFF BOUDICA, AND WILL THEN PROCEED TO THE AID OF LONDINIUM. WITH HIS 9TH LEGION TO DEFEND THEM, THE TOWN HAS NOTHING TO FEAR.

Catus Decianus was appalled at what was happening and realized things were out of his control. He knew only too well that someone was going to be blamed for all this. The most likely target for the anger of the people was the highest-ranking man in the city, so Catus Decianus decided he'd better make himself scarce. He packed his bags, got on his horse and headed for Gaul.

Those townsfolk who had the money, or who knew someone with a boat, swiftly followed Catus Decianus's example and left Londinium. The rest were left to defend themselves as best they could.

And still Boudica moved south, gathering support all the time. But her army was growing unwieldy. There were thousands and thousands of fighting men and women, and thousands of followers, too – the young, the old and the sick – some on horseback or driving chariots, but most on foot. The carts, which they'd used originally to transport the items they needed for day-to-day living, were even more heavily laden now – with looted goods. All this slowed down their progress, and gave time for word of the horrific destruction of Camulodunum to spread across the country.

An agonizing decision

The news of Boudica's bloodbath reached Governor Suetonius Paulinus on Mona. In shock and disbelief, he summoned a cavalry unit and headed at full speed down one of the finest Roman roads, Watling Street, towards Londinium. The rest of the army, the foot soldiers, were ordered to follow on behind.

121

Boudica and her army were feeling pretty confident now. After all, they'd managed to defeat the mighty Romans and burn their chief town. Anything else would be a doddle after that. They lingered on the journey, feasting and sharing tales of their battle deeds in the evenings, and generally taking things slowly.

They took things a little too slowly. The Britons could have covered the 60 or so miles to Londinium in three days if Boudica had felt any sense of urgency, but in the event, Suetonius Paulinus – travelling four times the distance – reached Londinium before them.

WAR REPORT
JULIUS AD 60
TO: THE EMPEROR OF ROME
FROM: SUETONIUS PAULINUS, GOVERNOR
OF BRITANNIA, AT LONDINIUM.

There is a very real threat that Boudica, Queen of the Iceni, will shortly enter Londinium with the sole purpose of destroying it. On hearing this, I, Suetonius Paulinus, rode from Mona to Londinium with a unit of cavalry, leaving my infantrymen to follow on at speed. The news of the complete destruction of Camulodunum has shattered the spirit of the people here. Many of the population of about 30,000 have already escaped

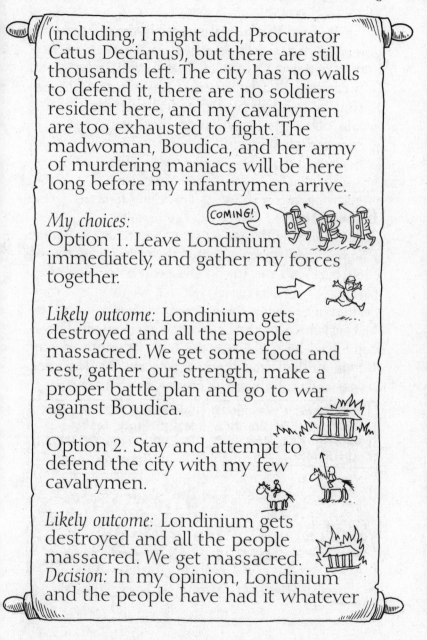

(including, I might add, Procurator Catus Decianus), but there are still thousands left. The city has no walls to defend it, there are no soldiers resident here, and my cavalrymen are too exhausted to fight. The madwoman, Boudica, and her army of murdering maniacs will be here long before my infantrymen arrive.

My choices:

(COMING!)

Option 1. Leave Londinium immediately, and gather my forces together.

Likely outcome: Londinium gets destroyed and all the people massacred. We get some food and rest, gather our strength, make a proper battle plan and go to war against Boudica.

Option 2. Stay and attempt to defend the city with my few cavalrymen.

Likely outcome: Londinium gets destroyed and all the people massacred. We get massacred.

Decision: In my opinion, Londinium and the people have had it whatever

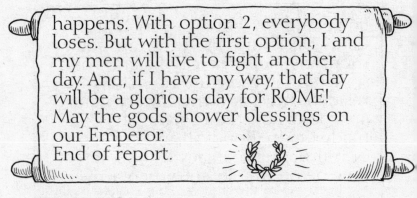

happens. With option 2, everybody loses. But with the first option, I and my men will live to fight another day. And, if I have my way, that day will be a glorious day for ROME! May the gods shower blessings on our Emperor.
End of report.

Evacuate!

To the horror of the residents of Londinium, Suetonius Paulinus and his men mounted their horses and turned their backs on the town. The people ran alongside, begging the soldiers to stay, not to leave them to certain death. But Suetonius Paulinus was a military man, and he had made his decision. By sacrificing Londinium, he was convinced he could save the rest of the province of Britain for the Roman Empire. And so, with despairing shrieks and wails ringing in his ears, he rode away.

Seeing that even the Roman soldiers feared Boudica, more people decided Londinium was an unhealthy place to be, and followed Suetonius Paulinus's small army up Watling Street. They reasoned that if Boudica followed them, the soldiers would be good for protection. Others, perhaps not fancying the long journey north, crossed the Thames and fled to find shelter with southern tribes who were still pro-Roman.

But some people who were too old or ill to travel, or just plain unwilling to leave their comfortable homes, stayed put. Within hours, they were dead.

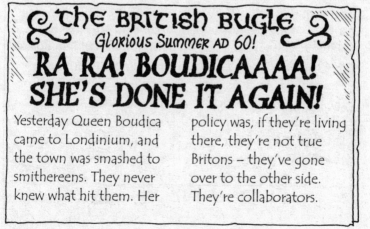

THE BRITISH BUGLE
Glorious Summer AD 60!
RA RA! BOUDICAAAA! SHE'S DONE IT AGAIN!

Yesterday Queen Boudica came to Londinium, and the town was smashed to smithereens. They never knew what hit them. Her policy was, if they're living there, they're not true Britons – they've gone over to the other side. They're collaborators.

So she came, she saw, and she conquered. Thanks to the dry weather we've been having, the whole place went up in smoke – whoosh! Bodies everywhere! Nothing escaped the wrath of the Queen. Her people rampaged through the town, swords slashing, daggers stabbing. Bodies swung from nooses at every corner. An eyewitness reports that when the British torched a warehouse full of grain, dozens of rats appeared from every crack in the walls. Along with the rats, men, women and children skittered this way and that, desperately trying to escape their attackers. Only the rats got away. Not a single human being was left alive. Decapitated bodies lay in the streets in pools of blood. The heads were taken to nearby streams as offerings to the gods.

It was Queen Boudica's order that no prisoners were to be taken. She could have sold prisoners of war as slaves and had a nice little income from it, but reports say that she didn't want to be hampered by chained prisoners when she moved on. Instead, she and her army helped themselves to all the food and wine they could manage.

There is no doubt that the army will move on and leave ash-covered Londinium behind. But to where? Will there be more plundering and killing, or has the Queen satisfied her thirst for revenge?

What next, Boudica?

SHE'S COMING – RUN!

Pockets of fighting began to break out all over the country. Perhaps the British people had heard news of the terrible, but successful, rebellion in the east. Maybe they thought that it was now or never. It was a good time to strike, while the Roman forces were weakened by having to rush all over the place, quelling rebellions as if they were stamping out small outbreaks of wildfire.

And while Boudica rambled up Watling Street, celebrating and looting on the way, Suetonius Paulinus, ahead of her, was making plans. But these were plans he daren't attempt to carry out without support. There wasn't time to send to Gaul for reinforcements, but there was one available unit that was nearer – the 2nd Legion.

You're on your own, Suetonius

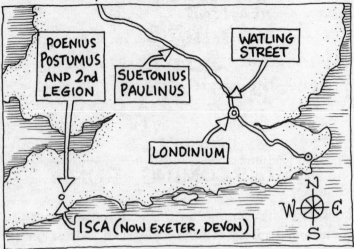

From: Suetonius Paulinus
To: Poenius Postumus, commander of the
2nd Legion, Isca Dumnoniorum
I salute you, Poenius Postumus, and ask for
your immediate assistance. Please send as
many cavalry and infantrymen as you
can spare to Watling Street. I can't pinpoint
our exact position, but we are moving north.
We have a large number of refugees from
Londinium with us, and are followed at
some distance by Queen Boudica and that
rabble she calls an army. Make no mistake,
they are great in number. My aim is to

regroup, rest my men and gather together as large a force as I can.

I look forward to seeing you and your men. Hurry, Poenius Postumus! We are waiting impatiently for you.

Suetonius Paulinus waited and waited for several days. Where was Poenius Postumus? There's no record of what decision Postumus made, or why he made it. Perhaps he was already fighting a battle with local tribespeople and was simply unable to get away.

Whatever the reason, the awful truth soon dawned on Suetonius Paulinus. Poenius Postumus wasn't coming. Nor was his army.

BOUDICA'S SECRET DIARY

SUMMER AD 60

Any respect I had for the Romans vanished in the smoke of Londinium. The cowards ran. Catus Decianus has gone, too. Good riddance. That vile man, who seized my daughters' rightful inheritance and drove me from my kingdom, has now been driven from his home. Or rather, he fled from his home, like a duck before a fox.

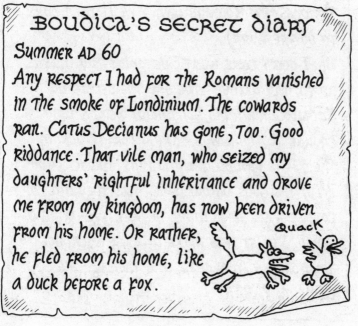

QUACK

If I know the Romans, his name will be mud - we won't hear anything of him ever again. But Suetonius Paulinus... I know he's not a coward. He's planning something, but what? We'll carry on following him up Watling Street, destroy his army before he has time to send for reinforcements, then throw the rest of the Romans out of Britain. After that, we can begin to get our country back on its feet and live the way we want to. We'll free the slaves (I mean the ones the Romans own - we'll need ours to do the work).

Oh, I don't care what Suetonius Paulinus is up to! My army - the one the people of Camulodunum and Londinium were stupid enough to think was barmy for attacking them - is far bigger than his. Braver, too! With the gods on our side - as they are, of course - we've nothing to fear. Speaking of which, I must now make a large sacrifice to the goddess Andraste, and then we are going to PARTY!

Queen Boudica's route was taking her straight towards the small country town of Verulamium, near present-day St Albans.

The population of Verulamium was mostly British: members of the Catuvellauni tribe, who'd grown to love the Roman style of life and all that went with it. They already had their own amphitheatre, and there were lots of new buildings going up, so Verulamium was a great place to raise a family. The land was fertile, and what the locals didn't grow for themselves was regularly delivered from all over the Empire. There were no soldiers camped nearby, so there wasn't much in the way of late-night rowdiness. It was a peaceful life.

But now, Queen Boudica's chariot rumbled towards them along Watling Street, the massive horde of Britons following behind.

A waiting game

Again, Suetonius Paulinus had to make an agonizing choice: whether to let the people of Verulamium suffer the same fate as those of Camulodunum and Londinium, or to lead his weary men into almost certain death.

He decided that it would be for the greater good to sacrifice Verulamium, and to stick to his original plan. When his men were in a safe location, they could be fed and rested. With their strength restored, and with their superior weapons, they would be more than a match for the rebels.

THE ROMAN SOLDIER...

...SIGNS UP FOR 25 YEARS. HE TRAINS PRACTICALLY EVERY DAY: RUNNING, SWIMMING, FENCING, JAVELIN-THROWING AND MARCHING.

...IS DISCIPLINED. IF HE DOESN'T FOLLOW ORDERS, HE'S LIKELY TO BE FLOGGED.

...BELONGS TO AN ORGANIZED ARMY. THEY KNOW EXACTLY WHO'S IN CHARGE. THEIR OFFICERS ARE EXPERIENCED, AND TRUSTED BY THEIR MEN.

...IS WELL-PAID. HE'S WELL-FED AND LOOKED AFTER. THE ROMAN ARMY'S NEVER SHORT OF BREAD, BUT HE DOES HAVE TO PAY FOR HIS FOOD.

...WEARS THE BEST ARMOUR AND UNIFORM IN THE WORLD AND CARRIES EXCELLENT WEAPONS. HE LOOKS AFTER HIS WEAPONS, SO THEY LOOK AFTER HIM.

...USES TRIED-AND-TESTED BATTLE TACTICS. HIS TRAINING MEANS HE KNOWS WHAT TO DO IN ANY SITUATION, WHOEVER HE'S FIGHTING. THAT GIVES HIM CONFIDENCE.

the celtic warrior...

...IS TRAINED FROM CHILDHOOD. HE DIDN'T HAVE A SOFT UPBRINGING LIKE ROMAN CHILDREN. HE'S BEEN FIGHTING AND USING WEAPONS SINCE HE WAS SMALL.

...CARRIES EXCELLENT WEAPONS. THE BRITISH METALWORKERS ARE AMONG THE BEST IN THE WORLD. THEIR WEAPONS ARE STRONG, RELIABLE AND FEARSOME.

...WEARS NO ARMOUR. HE FIGHTS BETTER WITHOUT CLOTHES AND ARMOUR WEIGHING HIM DOWN. HE RECKONS A MIGHTY WARRIOR HAS NO NEED OF ARMOUR, JUST SOME DECORATIONS IN WOAD.

...THINKS FOR HIMSELF. HE DOESN'T BOTHER WITH BATTLE PLANS. HE JUST HEADS INTO THE FIGHT AND GOES FOR IT. SURPRISE IS ONE OF HIS BEST WEAPONS.

133

Romans at the ready

Suetonius Paulinus moved his men north, out of the expected main trouble zone, convinced he'd made the right decision. And as his soldiers stepped up their daily training schedule and prepared their weapons for battle, the people of Verulamium were left to fend for themselves.

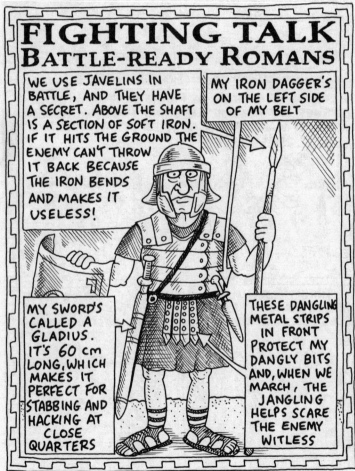

FIGHTING TALK
BATTLE-READY ROMANS

WE USE JAVELINS IN BATTLE, AND THEY HAVE A SECRET. ABOVE THE SHAFT IS A SECTION OF SOFT IRON. IF IT HITS THE GROUND THE ENEMY CAN'T THROW IT BACK BECAUSE THE IRON BENDS AND MAKES IT USELESS!

MY IRON DAGGER'S ON THE LEFT SIDE OF MY BELT

MY SWORD'S CALLED A GLADIUS. IT'S 60 cm LONG, WHICH MAKES IT PERFECT FOR STABBING AND HACKING AT CLOSE QUARTERS

THESE DANGLING METAL STRIPS IN FRONT PROTECT MY DANGLY BITS AND, WHEN WE MARCH, THE JANGLING HELPS SCARE THE ENEMY WITLESS

Vengeance at Verulamium

Boudica's army moved relentlessly forward. She and her daughters rode in their chariot, probably with a few heads strung from it. Behind her trundled thousands of heavily loaded carts, chariots, wagons and determined walkers.

It wasn't long, of course, before the people of Verulamium heard the news of Boudica's approach. And they knew it was bad news. After all, hadn't they been living almost as Romans for years? They could hardly expect mercy from someone who hated the occupying power with such a passionate loathing. And swarming along with the Iceni queen were the Trinovantes, the long-time enemies of the Catuvellauni. They, too, sought revenge.

Those Catuvellauni who could, fled. There were no great rivers to cross, no seas to take them away to another country. The people simply took to the hills, hid in the valleys, and burrowed deep into forests. But once again, for the elderly, for the very young or the sick, there was no escape. They were left alone to face certain death.

137

BOUDICA'S SECRET DIARY

LATE SUMMER AD 60

What a day! I'm totally worn out. My dress is absolutely crusty with blood, and it's beginning to smell like an old bone does when the dog's finished with it.

Verulamium was a piece of cake compared to Londinium and Camulodunum. Most of the people had already cleared off, but we burned their grain stores and fruit trees, and torched their crops. When – if – anyone returns, there'll be nothing left for them to eat. Let them starve. Who cares? As for the few thousand who stayed – we soon dealt with them. Traitors! Roman-lovers!

Verulamium itself didn't burn as easily as Londinium and Camulodunum. It had more stone buildings than anywhere I've ever seen – not temples, but ordinary people's houses. Roman-style houses, of course, so we smashed them up. Oh, we might have left a few bits of wall standing, but they're no use to anyone. LET THEM STAND FOR EVER – people can look at them and think, 'Queen Boudica was here. This is how she saved Britain from the giant clawing crab that was the Roman Empire.'

And now we're off north again. It amuses me to think that the Romans built WATLING STREET to help move their soldiers around quickly. Now it's helping a British army – the 'barmy' army that will destroy their own. For that is what I plan to do.

{ THE KILLING GROUND }

Suetonius Paulinus gathered together as many fighting men as he could. His force now consisted of the entire 14th Legion and a detachment of the 20th Legion. The legionaries were well-armed and well-trained Roman citizens, who were now at the peak of fitness and ready to go. He also had several thousand auxiliaries. These were soldiers who, because they were not citizens of Rome, but came from other provinces in the Roman Empire, were not eligible to be legionaries. Added to those were the cavalry – the horse-soldiers. In all, Suetonius Paulinus had between 10,000 and 13,000 men.

By now, he was resigned to the fact that he would never be able to match Queen Boudica's army for sheer size. But his men were highly disciplined, and would follow orders without question. With his brains and their fighting ability, he could do it! Suetonius Paulinus intended to use his vastly superior military experience to win this war.

A right site

Where the Britons had rambled around the country, fighting whenever and wherever they fancied, Suetonius Paulinus knew the value of choosing a battle site carefully. The right place would give his men the greatest advantage. Attacking Queen Boudica in open, flat countryside would be sheer suicide. The Brits would swarm all over the Romans like rats over a weak kitten. No, he had to find a site that would turn the one advantage Boudica had – sheer weight of numbers – into a handicap. However well his men fought, the Romans would have huge losses, he knew. Somehow he had to prevent the British masses making that deadly headlong rush. As his scouts scoured the countryside for the ideal place, he ordered his men to rest, eat and build up their strength, ready for what lay ahead.

Eventually, a battle site was found that suited Suetonius Paulinus's plans perfectly. It had a narrow valley which opened at the eastern end on to land that sloped gently down to the river. The valley had woodland on each side, and was backed by dense forest, all on steeply rising ground.

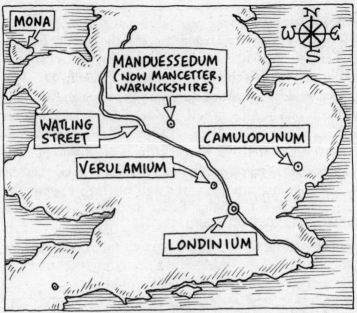

The site was near a Roman fort, so Suetonius Paulinus would have the added benefit of the extra fighting men who were stationed there as a peace-keeping force. He examined his battle site minutely, and was satisfied. Manduessedum it was.

BOUDICA'S SECRET DIARY

Late summer AD 60

Ha! I reckon we've got him cornered. Suetonius Paulinus is trying to hide from us against a forest on the other side of a river, but my scouts spotted a group of soldiers talking and swearing. Clots! They practically pointed out where the army's camped! Of course, Suetonius Paulinus could have set them up to do just that, but who cares? We know where they are, we outnumber them and our blood is up. This is it, Rome. When we've finished with your Governor, Britain will be ours once more, and you can get off our island and go and rule the rest of your rotten empire.

RIVER

The fool! When we cross the river and attack, he and his men will have nowhere to run to. I cannot believe that such an experienced soldier could have made such a simple mistake. But then, he probably feels that a so-called barmy army, led by a weak and feeble woman, can pose no threat to his mighty war machine.

We shall soon see. Tonight we rest. Tomorrow we ATTACK!

Battle-ready Brits

Boudica's army massed on flat, level ground on the eastern side of the river for the night, while Suetonius Paulinus occupied the western side.

Hundreds of carts and wagons were ranged several deep in a huge semicircle at the back of the British army. They were sited there so that all the people who weren't fighting could watch the battle, and be safely out of the way. Those who could, perched on top of their carts so they could get a good view.

It's possible that Boudica ordered the carts to be lined up like that. Maybe she just wanted everyone to have the chance to see the Brits scoring another victory over the Romans. Or maybe she wanted to block the way in case any of her warriors decided they'd rather run away, and live to fight again another day. After all, this was no town, open for burning and killing. This was something different. Instead of overrunning and slaughtering old people, small children and the sick, the Brits were about to take on the might of the Roman army – an army which was, this time, prepared for battle. Perhaps she realized that some of her people might be wondering if she'd bitten off more than she could chew.

Lull before the storm

Suetonius Paulinus was well aware that the Britons weren't an organized army. They wouldn't have a battle plan. As they had shown before, their tactics would be to try to terrify the enemy into running away.

But running away wasn't an option for the Romans. They had made a plan. And Suetonius Paulinus's choice of battleground was central to it. He'd considered that Boudica might send a section of her rabble round behind the Romans, to ambush them from the rear. The forest would prevent that. Only a few Britons would be able to get through at a time, and they would make so much noise that the Romans could pick them off at leisure.

OUCH!

No, all Suetonius Paulinus had to worry about was an attack from the front, from across the water. On the other side of the river were the Britons – as far as the eye could see. Smoke from their fires hung over the flat plain, looking for all the world like a gathering storm.

THE FINAL BATTLE!

Long before the battle began, the mass of Britons painted their bodies and faces with woad, and limed their hair, combing it into spikes that made them look taller and wilder. Some wore plaid trousers and tunics, some went naked. Those who had torcs wore them proudly. They ate and drank and waited. Gradually they became restless. Some began shrieking war-whoops, screaming and yelling at the Romans. More and more took up the cry until the din was deafening. The Brits were ready for war.

Speaking of war

It was time to call on the gods for support but, before that, Boudica planned to speak to her warriors, to encourage and inspire them. She mounted her chariot, and told her daughters to stand in front of her, so the people could see them, and would know that they were not afraid. Shaking the reins, she urged the horses on. The chariot rolled forward, carving a path through the massed warriors.

I HAVEN'T LED YOU HERE TO RECOVER A CROWN FOR MYSELF AND MY DAUGHTERS, OR TO WIN BACK THE PROPERTY THE ROMANS STOLE FROM ME. I'M HERE TO SEEK REVENGE FOR WHAT THEY DID TO MY BODY AND TO MY DAUGHTERS, AND TO SET MY PEOPLE FREE!

NO LONGER WILL ROMAN BOOTS WALK OVER US! WE HAVE ALREADY BEATEN ONE LEGION AND SENT THEIR CAVALRY SCURRYING TO SAFETY. WE HAVE DESTROYED THE TOWNS THEY BUILT.

LOOK! LOOK AT THEM! SEE HOW THEY CRINGE WITH TERROR AT OUR SHOUTS. IMAGINE HOW THEY'LL REACT WHEN WE ATTACK. NOW LOOK AT YOURSELVES. WE ARE THOUSANDS MORE THAN THEY ARE. WE ARE TRUE WARRIORS, NOT PAID SOLDIERS.

HERE, IN THE MIDDLE OF OUR LAND, WE MUST CONQUER THE INVADERS, OR DIE IN GLORY. THAT IS WHAT I WILL DO. IF YOU DO NOT THINK THE SAME, THEN YOU WILL LIVE IN SHAME AS SLAVES TO ROME.

LONG LIVE QUEEN BOUDICA!

YAY!

KILL THE ROMANS!

On the Roman side of the river, everything was ready. Suetonius Paulinus had lined up his men on the higher ground, so that the charging Britons would be below them. This would give the Romans an advantage, as it would be hard for the enemy to climb a slope and defend themselves at the same time.

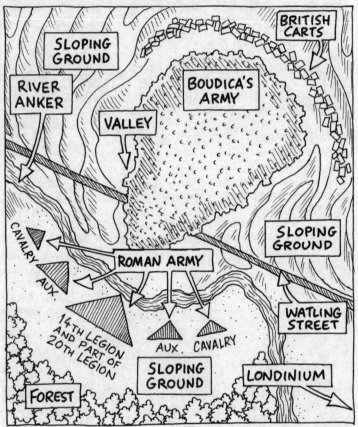

Before battle commenced, all Suetonius Paulinus had to do was fire up his men; he expected a lot from them and he had to make sure they were hungry for victory.

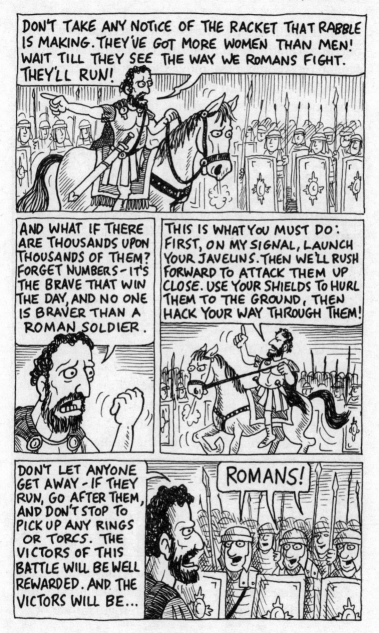

149

After their shouts, the Romans settled down into battle formation. Across the river, the Brits, in a screaming, yelling mass, moved forward. All the Druids among them moved to the front, towards the river bank. It was time to curse the enemy.

Death or glory

The Romans were all fired up, ready for war. As they shook their javelins and glowered at the enemy, Suetonius Paulinus saw that the time had almost come. He waited to give the signal to charge!

As the mass of Brits neared the Roman lines, they threw their spears wildly, then drew their swords, ready to hack and slash their way through the soldiers. However, as they approached the mouth of the valley, they hit trouble. The hills at each side prevented their onward charge. They had to press close together in order to get through the narrowing entrance.

The Romans didn't rush forward in a whirling mass. They advanced steadily, each legionary holding the first of his two javelins at the ready.

Whoosh! 7,000 javelins were launched through the air. Whoosh! 7,000 more.

The British were so tightly packed, that almost every javelin must have found a target.

THAT'S NOT GOOD FOR MUCH. WONDER IF HE KEPT THE RECEIPT.

Thousands of Britons died in the very first Roman javelin attack. The ones behind had to climb over their fallen comrades' bodies to get at their attackers. As they pushed forward into the valley, the sloping hillsides forced them ever closer together. Now it was impossible to use their long swords to any effect. Their chariots were worse than useless. The horses were unable to find space to move and soon became victims of the Roman onslaught. Chariots fell on their sides, tipping out their drivers and warriors.

Now the Romans, following Suetonius Paulinus's orders to the letter, closed up together and moved steadily and purposefully forward, using their shields to barge into the enemy. Now their gladii came into their own. The short swords were ideal for such close combat. Shove, stab, twist, pull ... shove, stab, twist, pull... They ploughed into and over the Brits and, once they'd moved out of the narrow valley entrance, the cavalry were able to come round and attack from the sides.

The Britons, trapped first between the hills on either side of the valley, and then by the cavalry cutting and slashing their way through them, had no option but to try to retreat. Most were pursued by the enemy and hacked down, but many made it back over the river, where they bolted across the plain, charging through their encampment, with the Romans close behind.

THE ROMAN MESSENGER

September AD 60

VICTORY!!!

Suetonius Paulinus 1: Boudica 0

NUMBERS HAVE YET TO BE CONFIRMED, BUT THERE'S NO DOUBT THAT THOUSANDS UPON THOUSANDS OF BRITONS DIED IN THE BATTLE OF MANDUESSEDUM – THE SO-CALLED 'PLACE OF CHARIOTS'. OUR ARMY DID US PROUD. SUETONIUS PAULINUS'S BATTLE PLAN PROVED THAT IT'S QUALITY NOT QUANTITY THAT COUNTS. NUMBERS WERE NO HELP AT ALL TO THE REBEL QUEEN BOUDICA. IT WAS EXPERIENCE, GOOD TRAINING AND DISCIPLINE THAT WON THE DAY.

ONCE THE REBELS REALIZED THEY COULD MAKE NO IMPACT ON OUR LEGIONS, THEY TURNED AND RAN LIKE FRIGHTENED HARES. BUT HERE THEY WERE FATALLY CAUGHT OUT BY THEIR OWN ARROGANCE. BEHIND THEIR SO-CALLED BATTLE LINES WERE RANGED HUNDREDS OF CARTLOADS OF LOOTED ROMAN AND ROMANO-BRITISH GOODS.

AND WITH THE CARTS WERE THEIR WARRIORS' FAMILIES AND SLAVES. THEIR AUDIENCE!

WELL, THIS WAS ONE SHOW THAT MADE THE HEADLINES – BUT NOT FOR THE REASONS THEY INTENDED. THE SEMICIRCLE OF VEHICLES AND ONLOOKERS CREATED A BARRIER THE FLEEING BRITS WERE UNABLE TO CROSS. THE CAVALRY RODE ALONG THEIR FLANKS, DRIVING THE ENEMY LIKE CATTLE, STRAIGHT INTO THE TRAP THEY'D CREATED FOR THEMSELVES. OUR SOLDIERS WERE ABLE TO PICK OFF THE BRITS AS THEY PLEASED – MEN, WOMEN, OLD, YOUNG, WARRIOR, SPECTATOR – EVERYONE.

THE REBELLION HAS BEEN CRUSHED. NOT ONE OF THE REBELS WAS ALLOWED TO LIVE TO RISE AGAIN. ROMAN BRITAIN, YOU ARE SECURE! SLEEP SOUNDLY IN YOUR BEDS TONIGHT.

OUR BOYS HAD PLENTY TO CELEBRATE LAST NIGHT!

ᴛhe BRITISh BUGLe
Final Edition AD 60
AD 60
EMERGENCY EDITION

All true Britons are mourning the loss of thousands of our men and women: husbands, wives, fathers, mothers, sons and daughters. The slaughter by the Roman imperialists must surely go down in history as an all-time tragedy. This is our land.

Our people fought only for what is theirs by right.

We urge our people to accept that Queen Boudica is lost to us. The Romans have triumphed. These are dark days indeed for Britain.

But – if the Romans think that this is over, then they are fools. One day, the invaders will be driven from Britain. And when they are, we will wipe all trace of them from the face of the land.

Missing queen

There were no confirmed sightings of Queen Boudica, or of her daughters. Rumours flew throughout the land.

Dio Cassius tells us that Boudica was captured by the Romans, and that she became seriously ill and died. Her body, he says, was buried with ceremony and honour, and at great expense. He doesn't mention her daughters.

Tacitus, however, has another story. He wrote that Boudica committed suicide by taking a dose of poison. In normal circumstances, she and her daughters – if they had survived the battle – might have expected to be taken back to Rome as prisoners. There they would be paraded before the Roman citizens, and enslaved. It's probable that Boudica could not tolerate such shame and, believing that she would go to a better world after death, preferred to kill herself – and maybe her daughters, too.

It's entirely possible that Boudica and her daughters were brutally slain on the battlefield and that, amid so many bodies, and so much blood and gore, it was impossible to find them. No body has ever been found.

AFTER BOUDICA

So ended the year AD 60. With Boudica's death, British hopes of self-rule died, too. Their Druid stronghold on Mona had been completely destroyed, and they had no great leader.

Despite their final triumph at Manduessedum, the Roman army's pride must have been badly battered. They'd been unable to prevent a woman from destroying the three biggest towns in the land, and they'd lost thousands of their own people to a horde of undisciplined barbarians.

Things looked pretty bleak for the Brits who were left. They could only expect harsh treatment from the angry Romans.

Suetonius Paulinus took his revenge on the Iceni, among whom the whole rebellion had begun. He moved in on Iceni territory in a big way, building forts and firmly establishing a strong Roman presence. Tacitus says that the British had been so sure they could wipe out the Romans and take all their food, that they hadn't bothered to do the usual annual planting. But it's also possible that Suetonius Paulinus simply took the Iceni's stores, and damaged their crops, hoping to starve them into submission.

Meanwhile, Nero sent an official to check out the state of things in Britain. Suetonius Paulinus was still wreaking revenge, but had also made the mistake of losing a few expensive Roman ships, complete with crews so, in AD 61, he was ordered to hand over his job and the army to a new governor, Publius Petronius Turpilius, who worked hard to calm things down on the island. The Iceni were eventually given their own land, called Venta Icenorum. It was at a place we know today as Caistor, near Norwich, in Norfolk. Within a generation or two, the British people accepted Roman ways, and grew to appreciate the benefits of their more advanced civilization. This civilization lasted for another 350 years and, as it prospered, Boudica's name was gradually forgotten.

A name to remember

But 1,000 years later in the 16th century, when Elizabeth I was on the throne, more and more people came to know of Boudica through reading the Latin writings of Tacitus and Dio Cassius, which had been rediscovered. Myths and legends began to spring up about this fearsome British woman who was, like their own queen, a redhead.

Celtic lore

Boudica or Boadicea?

There was confusion over Boudica's name. Examples of the ancient word for 'victory' have been found that show it to be spelt with one 'c', but Tacitus spelt it with two: Boudicca. Then in the Middle Ages someone got a bit sloppy with his spelling. The 'u' was changed to an 'a', and a letter 'c' to an 'e', and suddenly she was known as Boadicea.

By the time Victoria was on the throne in the 19th century, Boudica was firmly established as Boadicea. The Victorians loved that name. They thought it was romantic, and the meaning of 'victory' matched their own queen's name.

VERY NICE, MA'AM

That wasn't the only confusion over Boudica's name. At different times, she's been known as Boudiga (also the name of a Celtic goddess), Bunduca, Bonduica, Voadicea and the rather glamorous Boodicia. Even today, Boudica is often spelled Boudicca.

In 1902, the statuesque warrior queen was commemorated in a statue on the Embankment by Westminster Bridge, in London. Sharp knives are shown sticking out from the wheels of Boudica's chariot – just one of the legends that have grown up around the lady.

Legends tell of Boudica being buried at Stonehenge, or on London's Hampstead Heath – even under one of the platforms of London's King's Cross Station.

There is no marked grave. All we have are the histories of Roman writers, and a name – a name that is still remembered nearly 2,000 years after the death of Queen Boudica.